the happy index

james timpson

the happy index

lessons in upside-down management

Harper
North

HarperNorth
Windmill Green
24 Mount Street
Manchester M2 3NX

A division of
HarperCollins*Publishers*
1 London Bridge Street
London SE1 9GF

www.harpercollins.co.uk

HarperCollins*Publishers*
Macken House
39/40 Mayor Street Upper
Dublin 1
D01 C9W8

First published by HarperNorth in 2024

3 5 7 9 10 8 6 4 2

A catalogue record for this book
is available from the British Library

The Happy Index contains updated material that was originally
published as part of the author's *Sunday Times* column in 2020.

HB ISBN: 978-0-00-865474-0
TPB ISBN: 978-0-00-865475-7

Printed and bound in the UK using 100%
renewable electricity at CPI Group (UK) Ltd, Croydon

To Roisin,
whose kindness and compassion
inspires me every day.

CONTENTS

CONTENTS

CONTENTS

CONTENTS

INTRODUCTION

*Outlining an Upside-Down
Approach to Management*

I've been very lucky to have a boss (who also happens to be my dad), who believes in our culture of trust and kindness completely, and has supported me as I've learned how to lead. My dad, John, is the perfect boss to have. I've also been incredibly fortunate to work with so many amazing colleagues who have decided that Timpson is a good place to spend the majority of their careers. These colleagues, who many of you won't ever meet or know, are the rock of our company, and the custodians of our culture. Many of us have grown up together, and worked hard to develop a culture that most people thought would fail. They walk the walk, and I'm proud to have them as colleagues.

If you visit one of our shops to get a key cut or your shoes repaired, you will hopefully be met by a smiling colleague, who is happy to be there to serve you. In many ways it's a pretty simple business. We usually have only one colleague in each shop, our stock never goes out of date, and we have no technology to worry about. But to make it into a simple business has taken decades of work, developing a unique culture where trust and kindness is at its core.

The shoe repair business isn't necessarily the first industry that springs to mind when you think of a workplace full of innovation, excitement, and surprises. I'm here to tell you though, that the way we do things at Timpson is far from boring, and despite being founded in 1865, we aren't a traditional company at all.

If you dig a little deeper into how we do things, you will find that there's a lot more than the day-to-day operations of getting shoelaces, rubber heels, and key blanks to the 2,100 branches that I oversee in my role as CEO. In fact, we rarely talk about the nuts and bolts of getting the shops open and the money in the till. Instead, we talk about the two most important factors in running a business: people and culture. If we get these right, we make money.

From its very beginning, Timpson has forever been a company brimming with entrepreneurial spirit. Our story began with the vision and determination of William Timpson, the founder of the company that I oversee today. Born in 1849, my great-great-grandfather displayed an innate business eye from a young age, crafting and selling leather boot laces from when he was just eight years old. As a child, he would carry boots from Rothwell in Northamptonshire to the bustling boot factory in neighbouring Kettering for repairs – a journey of five miles and not an easy route for a young lad.

At the age of 16, he travelled to Manchester, where he worked alongside his older brother Charles, delivering boots throughout the city. After a falling out with Charles, William returned to Rothwell, where he later took over the business of an elderly shoe repairer after the owner had passed away.

In 1865, William made the journey back to Manchester, where he opened his own retail boot and shoe business at 97 Oldham Street, the very first Timpson branch. This was just the beginning of the extraordinary journey that would see the Timpson family business flourish into what it is today. William's dedication to his craft paved the way for the establishment of a warehouse in Great Ducie Street, Manchester, in 1895, capable of housing a staggering – for its day – 40,000 pairs of shoes.

Since then, the Timpson legacy has continued through the generations, with William's son, William Henry Farey Timpson, becoming Managing Director in 1912. Despite his declining health, William Timpson senior continued to make frequent trips from Kettering to Manchester to visit the warehouse and keep an eye on the business.

After William died in 1929, his philanthropic efforts lived on, deeply intertwined with the community. The local residents of Kettering, where he was laid to rest, displayed their respect for him by lining the streets in silent tribute and closing their shops on the Saturday.

Fast forward to the present day, and we find ourselves in a new era here at Timpson. My great-great-grandfather's determination and graft has been passed down through the generations, to become one of the most successful and well-recognized brands that continues to serve its customers to this day. People are at the heart of everything we do, and it is those individuals who have transformed Timpson from a local shoe business serving its regional customers into a nationwide company.

Over the past 25 years, we have expanded into more shops and more services, increasing sales to over £300 million, and profits to over £40 million, despite being in an industry suffering from terminal decline. And, of course, I've failed many times, and made countless mistakes along the way, but, most importantly, through failing I've learned that the way to survive in business is to lead with kindness. This simple strategy is at the root of everything we do, and goes a long way to ensuring you get great service in our shops, from colleagues who are happy to be there. The happier they are, the better we seem to do.

You would have thought that as CEO of a retail business I would spend hours on end looking over reports that capture the sales data from each of the branches that we manage (we don't digitise our sales data from tills, which, as I will explain later, is for a very simple reason). I don't. Instead I look at a report that comes out on a Thursday night that tells me how happy colleagues are. Not surprisingly this is the best barometer to judge how well the sales are going, and how well customers are being served. We do zero market research, never have a budget meeting, nor borrow money from a bank. We just focus on how we can inspire happy colleagues.

As you will find, I very rarely spend much time in our offices as I am often travelling up and down the country visiting our branches. I set off early as I like to get to the first shop of the day before it opens. I don't tell anyone where I'm going but by the end of the day the jungle drums have gone off, and the element of surprise diminishes. Visiting shops and talking to colleagues is the best part of the job, and it teaches you that the answers to your problems aren't found by sitting behind a desk, but by asking the people who run the business – our colleagues.

Typically, when our sales have dropped it is because one of our colleagues has encountered a problem, which usually has nothing to do with their job and is often beyond their control. It is this area where we – I firmly believe – offer stand-out care. It is our duty to try and help colleagues navigate a way out of any difficult situations, be it personal or professional. It's good for them and it's good for business.

I have never been a fan of job descriptions, which I will discuss in **Lesson One** (see page 13), but if I had one, my biggest responsibility as CEO would be to care for our colleagues. This goes ahead of everything else (shareholder value, profit targets, market share, the level of dividends, and so on), because colleagues *always* come first. While I am very commercially minded, I have learned that if our colleagues don't come first you won't achieve the financial results that you had hoped for. Even the most capable people can have an off period, and in helping someone get back on track, you will find far more enjoyment than paying a bumper dividend, and the financial benefits are clear. People who are cared for give you their best.

Towards the end of each month, I receive a confidential report (called 'Colleagues of Concern'), which outlines three key areas: mental wellbeing, physical health, financial worries. Some colleagues are on the list just once, while others struggle over many years. Either way it's our job to help. If we don't, we could potentially lose some of the best people in the business.

There are many ways we can support, but rarely is money the only answer. We have a whole toolbox of ways we can help, but the most important is the time we give to talk and show kindness. Being kind doesn't mean we're a pushover, but it is the most commercially effective tool a leader can use. It's surprising how few organizations see this.

Like many other businesses around the globe, the past two decades have been littered with situations that were difficult to navigate, including increased living costs, global recessions, a worldwide pandemic (when we nearly ran out of money), the influence of AI, and more. However, what has been the driving force of our company during these periods of uncertainty is the consistency of the people who manage our branches up and down the country, and the culture in which they work. Great people always help you weather the storms.

Using the lessons contained within *The Happy Index*, I will provide you with the tools that can help your business grow, share insights into the dos and don'ts of a happy workplace, and give you a different perspective on how to lead, and lead in a way that's fun! Whether you're a CEO, project leader, supervisor, new joiner, or anything else in between, this book is for you, whatever stage you're at in your career.

The Happy Index has been written so that you can read the lessons in any order. Say, for example, that you're struggling to find the words for that difficult conversation with a member of your team, or are finding it hard to get time off because of personal problems, then **Lesson Seven** (see page 217) might be the section for you to turn to first.

Below, you will find a brief outline of what you can expect to learn from each of the lessons.

Lesson One: Assemble a High-Performing Super Team and You Will Never Have to Worry

- Explore unconventional methods of recruiting based on personality and potential, not just qualifications. A CV can be a waste of time.

- Embrace diversity by hiring from varied backgrounds for a more inclusive and successful team.
- Maintain high workplace standards to enhance business success, customer satisfaction, and brand reputation.

Lesson Two: If You Build It, They Will Come – How to Have a Great Company Culture

- Transform your office environment to support employee wellbeing and health, creating a positive culture so people want to work at the office, not from home.
- Introduce initiatives like office gyms, free fruit, cost price office restaurants, and wellbeing app subscriptions to foster a culture of care and support for your employees' physical and mental health.
- Demonstrate your commitment to employee wellbeing by offering additional days off for special life events, allowing people to prioritize their health and work-life balance.

Lesson Three: To Get Ahead, You've Got to Get About

- Looking at the competition can help your company gain valuable insights and strategies to enhance your services, which can lead to increased customer satisfaction and improved business performance.
- Embracing change while staying true to your core values can make your business more resilient. This adaptability can help your company navigate challenges effectively and maintain a strong market position.
- When employees are happy, they are more engaged, and this positively impacts your business's success and reputation.

Lesson Four: The State and the Street: A Story of Government and Business

- Learn how government policies can promote an equal treatment of suppliers, regulate retailer–supplier relationships, and prevent practices that only serve the few, benefiting businesses through a fair competitive environment.
- Understand the pivotal role of landlords on the high street and how government encouragement can lead to flexibility for this key partnership, creating stable and supportive conditions for businesses across the country.
- Discover the challenges of government intervention and how to avoid unintended consequences, ensuring that regulations aimed at revitalizing high streets do not burden businesses, providing a balanced and regulated framework for sustainable growth.

Lesson Five: Succession Planning and the Future of Your Business

- Learn how 'strategic planning' is not just a buzzword but a critical component for thriving in the contemporary business environment. Discover the importance of setting clear goals that are simple and achievable with hard work and a little bit of good luck. As well as ongoing strategy evaluation for sustained success in the future of your own business.
- Understand how innovation plays a pivotal role in propelling any enterprise forward and how these actions can drive your company to new heights, from the value of

embracing fresh ideas and cultivating a creative culture to daring to innovate.

- Discover that adaptability is not only about surviving but thriving in a world that continually changes around you. Explore how companies that can pivot swiftly, learn from challenges, and maintain agility are better prepared to navigate the uncertainties of the future, providing insights for your business's growth and longevity.

Lesson Six: Lead by Example

- Learn how leadership shapes a culture of kindness by prioritizing the wellbeing of employees and customers.
- Master the art of using straightforward language for better understanding, culture alignment, and increased productivity, even when it means saying no.
- Understand the critical process of promoting colleagues into leadership roles and, crucially, how leaders should provide guidance and advice for a smoother transition, creating higher chances of success for individuals already within the company.

Lesson Seven: Navigating Difficult Situations in the Workplace

- Learn the value of focusing on areas of expertize and avoiding over-diversification in your business.
- Understand the importance of rethinking rigid rules to promote workplace creativity and trust among employees.
- Master the skills of clear communication during challenging conversations, leading to better relationships and outcomes in your business.

Lesson Eight: Give Back to Get More

- Learn the value of hiring individuals who deserve a second chance, unlocking hidden potential in your team and contributing to safer communities.
- Understand the positive impact of supporting colleagues in giving back to the underprivileged, providing assistance to those in need, and enhancing happiness within your company.
- Explore the benefits of early training investments for various at-risk groups, fostering a culture of learning, training and volunteering that gives back to wider society.

As you journey through these lessons, you'll find a wealth of real-world examples and concise takeaways to guide you on your quest for a happier, more successful workplace and team. Don't worry if you can't remember something from any of the lessons as there will be summary points at the end of each section for you to easily refer to.

Let's get stuck in!

ASSEMBLE A HIGH-PERFORMING SUPER TEAM AND YOU WILL NEVER HAVE TO WORRY

Welcome to **Lesson One**, where we will look at the secrets behind assembling a high-performing Super Team. We will look at the differences in recruitment, from more nuanced personal approaches to science-based models that all aim to recruit exceptional individuals and cultivate an environment that will allow every team member to thrive. A happy team is a high-performing team.

The task of assembling a Super Team is a multifaceted one, necessitating a thoughtful approach that goes beyond the confines of conventional recruitment methods. In the following lesson, we will explore Timpson's unique methodology – a methodology that marries the selection of exceptional talent with a profound commitment to the wellbeing of each team member.

I will keep saying it until I am blue in the face: at the heart of every successful venture lies a remarkable, happy team. Far beyond strategies and bottom lines, it's the collective spirit, expertize, and dedication of individuals that propel businesses to greatness. Looking forward to going to work every day should be a normal way of life.

Recruitment, often seen as a never-ending puzzle for businesses, should focus on personality, not qualifications. We'll look at the intricacies of a more personal, face-to-face approach, understanding how unconventional methods can unearth exceptional talent that traditional hiring practices might overlook, and I will show you how to apply our very own, tailor-made 'Cobbler Algorithm' to your business.

Hiring the right people and building your business from there is just the beginning to a organization's success, and things have moved on a fair bit since my great-great-grandfather set up our company in 1865. In order to be the best, we need to find the best people, but we also need to look to non-traditional hiring pools to secure those individuals; it's about tapping into a pool of dedicated, hardworking individuals who can reshape the future of your organization, not judging them because of x, y, and z. Relying on a computer to select your people isn't, in our view, a wise approach.

Let's bring that Super Team together.

WRITING THE PERFECT CV

Now, before we start talking about the best ways to hire people I'd like you to perform a quick exercise. Using either the blank page here or a piece of paper that you have to hand, I'd like you to spend 60 seconds writing down the most crucial aspects of a CV that you think a hiring manager needs to see, ahead of offering you a time for a job interview.

Before you begin though, really think about what you need to add to the page to give yourself the best shot.

My CV

Great, now that you've done that, turn over the page to see what we, at Timpson, are looking for when we're offering interviews to potential candidates.

The most important details to have on your CV

- Your name
- Your contact details

That's right! It's just your name and your contact details. I can imagine that some of you might feel a bit cheated here and, if that's the case, I apologize. But what I want you to know about our company is that we don't care about your previous experience, the skills you've acquired along the way, what your past says about you, or any qualifications that you might have picked up over the years. A university degree is a great achievement, but it's irrelevant when it comes to what we are looking for.

If you're interested in working for us, the only things we need to know about you are your name and how best to contact you. Everything else is about you and the personality that you have, which leads me on nicely to ...

HOW DO YOU RECRUIT THE MOST TALENTED PEOPLE?

The pursuit of employment puts job seekers in their most vulnerable state; a feeling that is often exacerbated by automated recruitment systems, clunky online applications, and the discouraging silence from companies that opt not to respond. This disjointed experience tarnishes employers' reputations, prompting a need for a more considerate and personal approach to recruitment. A feasible alternative exists – one that fosters positive impressions even if faced with a rejection. While the allure of technology to filter applications is clear, a more laborious yet rewarding path lies in ignoring what's written in a CV and speaking to people face-to-face, to judge if their personality is one that will thrive in our culture. This way we also find candidates from diverse backgrounds, irrespective of the perceived blemishes in their lives. The qualities that truly distinguish exceptional candidates are not spotless academic results, nor perfect references, but rather the intangibles of personality and vitality. If you leave it to a computer to filter the applications, you will end up interviewing the same kind of people over and over again.

Within the recruitment landscape, intricate algorithms have emerged, ostensibly designed to filter through applications and identify suitable matches, all without recruiters ever laying eyes on the applicants themselves. Requirements such as a 2.1 degree rather than a 1st, a Duke of Edinburgh Gold Award, and an A* in Maths A Level become the deciding factors that lead to an interview. Candidate names are fed into the system, initiating a cycle of communication, interviews and, ultimately, the selection of one or two almost indistinguishable candidates.

Arctic Shores, a trailblazing recruitment technology business, is at the forefront of innovation, applying 'gamified psychometrics' grounded in cognitive neuroscience to uncover top-tier talent. While this approach lies beyond familiar terrain and raises concerns for individuals who might not thrive in such an environment, its potential impact is undeniable. Their approach involves evaluating candidates' skills through online games, transforming the recruitment process into an engaging, dare I say, 'enjoyable' journey. However, in stark contrast to this trajectory stands the ethos at Timpson, a beacon of distinct practice. Here, a *curriculum vitae* serves just two functions: it reveals the applicant's name and phone number. These are the only details you need.

A notable aspect of Timpson's recruitment method is that many recruits never submit a traditional CV at all. Instead, they come recommended to us by friends or family members attuned to the company's desired personality traits and job requirements. Over a quarter of our company joined us this way. The approach, coupled with a £250 bonus incentive, ensures a steady stream of potential candidates. We do use online job boards like everyone else to advertise our vacancies, but we find that it's better to look elsewhere to find the best people.

The subsequent phase of recruiting great people involves what we internally refer to as the Cobbler Algorithm, which translates into having meaningful conversations performed over phone calls or through a face-to-face meeting.

A determining factor in the selection for Timpson is an applicant's personality. Skills like key cutting and shoe repair can be taught, but moulding one's personality remains beyond the realm of training. We could teach you to repair a watch in a week, but we couldn't train you to be someone you aren't. This is the same for any job requiring hands-on knowledge. Consequently, the focus in our screening of candidates' suitability shifts towards identifying happy, energetic, funny, and idiosyncratic individuals; traits that directly correlate with future success within the company.

This initial assessment is performed during a brief 15-minute conversation, a foundational filter that determines those candidates worthy of progressing to the next stage: a paid trial day. This trial serves as a mutual exploration of compatibility. In this phase, the evaluation of an applicant's personality fit relies on an intuitive, gut-based rating, which might be simplistic, but has proven effective. I'm often amazed that candidates coming to the office for an interview don't realize that the most important test is how they interact with Paul and Lauren on reception, before we've even met them. I'm a believer that people who are chatty and friendly to strangers make the best colleagues.

The scale of personality assessment at Timpson ranges from 1 to 10, with scores of 9 or 10 indicating a strong match. It's easy to spot someone who is a 5 out of 10 or less, as well as the 9s and 10s, but there is a common problem we have to battle against. The danger zone is when you believe someone is within the zone of 6s, 7s, and 8s. While these candidates meet the minimum criteria, they do not align with the elevated standards upheld by Timpson. They are simply not good enough to work alongside our amazing colleagues. Interestingly, the investment required to train and integrate a new colleague, whether exceptional or subpar, is almost exactly the same, which means we only want to spend time selecting the best from the pool.

Inspired by a 2007 visit to the Southwest Airlines offices in Love, Texas, the seeds of Timpson's transformative recruitment method were sown. The visit illuminated the significance of building a robust team before embarking on the journey ahead. In the context of an airline, a right number of people, including pilots, crew, and ground personnel, is essential for take-off – an absent crew member causes the entire operation to fail. To counter this challenge, Southwest employed a straightforward tool: a waiting list of great people who are perfect to join when a role becomes available, so they didn't have to worry about gaps in their people line up. They have a great phrase at Southwest ... 'we're only making money when the wheels are up'. They know to get the planes in the air they need a complete team of great people who are trained in what they're doing. Any gaps mean the planes can't fly, so always have a line-up of great people on the bench.

This simple yet ingenious concept now lies at the core of Timpson's recruitment strategy. The company focuses on identifying exceptional candidates brimming with personality who are willing to wait until a suitable vacancy arises. By sidestepping the pressure to hastily fill positions, this approach prevents the compromise of hiring mediocre candidates, and instead nurtures a pool of highly talented individuals eager to join the team. When you're desperate, you lower the bar.

However, the most challenging aspect of the recruitment role remains delivering the news of unsuccessful applications. Engaging in such conversations requires a unique brand of empathy – one that acknowledges the candidate's vulnerability and respects their investment in the process. Instead of resorting to automated, impersonal emails, Timpson advocates for compassionate responses, coupled with constructive career advice. This approach recognizes the long-term implications of rejection; today's applicants could very well be tomorrow's customers. Therefore, every interaction with an applicant becomes an opportunity to demonstrate our internal commitment to humanity and respect.

Reflecting on my own experiences with job rejections following my graduation from university in the mid-nineties, I remember how these interactions influenced my perception of the various companies I had applied to work for. The memories of well-handled rejections linger, shaping my spending choices, while the poorly managed ones are best forgotten. This dynamic underscores the symbiotic relationship between recruitment, customer relations, and the inherent humanity within each interaction, setting the stage for a more equitable and compassionate employment landscape. It's hard for a computer to manage this with kindness.

The Cobbler Algorithm and Personality Criteria

Score	Qualities
10	Energetic and exceptional, they leave a lasting impact and are open to change.
9	Outstanding and enthusiastic, with room for improvement but reliable and open to growth.
6–8	Decent but average, they tick a lot of the boxes but may lack long-term commitment. Their best isn't good enough for our amazing colleagues to work alongside them. When you're desperate to recruit they seem better than they really are.
5	Average, necessitating substantial HR management and unlikely to excel.
3–4	Below average, challenging to work with, and likely to be unreliable and perform poorly, posing HR issues down the line.
1–2	An HR Director's nightmare, to be avoided at all costs.

It's essential to understand that even in the best organizations, some employees might at some point exhibit negative traits due to external pressures in their life.

OUR EASY METHOD FOR UNDERSTANDING CANDIDATES

In my journey as a business leader, I've come to deeply appreciate the immense value of hiring a diverse range of people. The true strength of a team lies in its diversity, not only in terms of race, gender, or background but also in the skills and qualities that each individual brings to the table. At Timpson, when we embark on the hiring process, we don't just focus on qualifications and experience; we also consider the characters listed in our *Mr. Men*-inspired table (below) as a framework for evaluating candidates.

The decision to prioritize diversity in our hiring practices is rooted in the belief that all individuals' unique perspectives and skills are like pieces of a puzzle that need to fit together to make the right picture. When you assemble a team, it's like creating a complex jigsaw, and every piece plays a crucial role in forming the complete picture. Just like how our Cobbler Algorithm allows us to assess candidates on a 1–10 scale based on their personality and suitability for the job, these characters, inspired by the well-loved children's book series *Mr. Men*, adds an additional layer to our evaluation process.

Each character in the table below embodies a distinct set of qualities, and we look for elements of these traits in candidates to ensure we have a well-rounded and dynamic team.

CANDIDATE EVALUATION FRAMEWORK

Character	Key traits
Mr Keen	Trustworthy, Customer-Centric, Collaborative, Service-Oriented, Adaptable
Mr Reliable	Dependable, Diligent, Caring, Loyal, Honest
Mrs Determined	Resilient, Goal-Oriented, Problem-Solver, Confident, Persistent
Ms Meticulous	Detail-Oriented, Organized, Analytical, Thorough
Mr Hard-working	Diligent, Committed, Persevering, Conscientious, Results-Oriented
Miss Helpful	Supportive, Kind, Collaborative, Empathetic, Customer-Focused
Mrs Conscientious	Detail-Oriented, Methodical, Reliable, Ethical, Organized
Mr Successful	Achievement-Oriented, Ambitious, Results-Driven, Visionary, Decisive
Mrs Ambitious	Aspiring, Goal-Oriented, Driven, Determined, Visionary

When hiring, it's crucial to identify and address negative traits to ensure the right fit for the organization. Candidates displaying negative characteristics like those listed below might not be the best fit. Interviewers should be wary of these traits, in combination with the Cobbler Algorithm, to not only evaluate positive qualities but also flag any undesirable behaviours like those listed here.

Character	Key traits
Mr Scruffy	Unkempt, Unreliable, Disorganized
Ms Late	Punctually Challenged, Unreliable
Mr Is-it-Five-o'Clock?	Clock-watcher, Unmotivated, Unengaged
Mr Rude	Disrespectful, Inconsiderate, Impolite
Mr Careless	Negligent, Inattentive, Haphazard
Miss Don't Care	Apathetic, Disinterested, Unmotivated
Mr Grumpy	Irritable, Negative, Unpleasant
Mr Dull	Boring, Uninspiring, Unmotivated
Mrs Slow	Inefficient, Lackadaisical, Lethargic
Mr Scrounger	Lazy, Opportunistic, Unreliable
Mr Dishonest	Untrustworthy, Deceptive, Unreliable
Miss Fib	Dishonest, Unreliable, Untrustworthy

Sometimes, you might have hired someone who was brilliant on the day but then, after a while, they might suddenly start displaying traits and characteristics from the negative traits table. However, if this happens it's essential to understand that even in the best organizations, some employees might at some point exhibit negative traits due to external pressures in their life. Instead of dismissing them outright, it's more beneficial to address these issues delicately, and with an openness that allows them to feel comfortable talking about stressors in their lives outside of work. Managers should remind these employees of their valuable skills, and give them opportunities to improve. Everyone can have off days, or phases where they exhibit less-than-ideal qualities. By offering support and guidance, you might help them rediscover their positive traits, and regain their enthusiasm and motivation once again.

Our overall approach is not to stigmatize any colleagues but, instead, give them the help they need to grow and thrive within the business. By maintaining an understanding and support-ive environment, companies can address and overcome negative traits, fostering personal and professional develop-ment among their team members.

By evaluating candidates based on the characteristics listed on page 27, we are able to build a team that is not just diverse in terms of skills but also in terms of their personal attributes. We understand that it's the blend of qualities and experiences that create a dynamic Super Team, not how many qualifica-tions a person has.

When we hire a diverse range of individuals with different strengths and qualities, we are able to create an environment of true innovation and collaboration. It's about constructing a team that can effectively tackle challenges from various angles, see opportunities that others may miss, and work together harmoniously. In a world that's constantly evolving, this diver-sity ensures our adaptability and resilience to face whatever may be around the corner.

Ultimately, hiring based on both qualifications and charac-ter allows us to create a workplace that reflects the rich tapestry of human abilities and experiences. It's this approach that has helped us not only survive but thrive, providing our customers with exceptional service, and our team with a fulfilling work environment. At Timpson, we understand that it's our people who make the difference, and embracing their diverse quali-ties is what propels us forward.

A FRESH START: THE BENEFITS OF EMPLOYING EX-OFFENDERS

During my childhood, my mum Alex, a foster carer, would take us to HMP Styal, a women's prison near Manchester. I would sit in the car, gazing through the window at the towering fence, while she brought the babies she cared for inside to visit their incarcerated mothers.

Travelling to prisons has become a regular fixture in my schedule. Most weeks I visit prison wings, talking with inmates and seeking out vibrant personalities to join our retail business. Initially, I had the privilege of handpicking exceptional candidates without much competition. However, other employers have recognized the potential of this approach in unearthing talent and granting individuals a second chance at life. Companies that once shied away from association with ex-offenders now welcome them with open arms. By embracing prison leavers, companies widen their chances of finding great people. Just recently, our recruitment team arrived at a prison only to discover that Greggs the bakery chain had been there recruiting the week before, and hired all the best people. Good on them!

I am driven by wanting to run a highly profitable business, and I know the only way I can do this is to have the best people. It's the same in most walks of life; the team that wins the football tournament is likely to also have the best players. This is why over 10 per cent of my colleagues come directly from prison. We find that 'returning citizens' are often the most dedicated, honest, and hardworking colleagues we can find – many of them are still incarcerated, but they participate on day release, working in our shops and supporting us from the office. This week, I encountered a colleague who, before incarceration, had been a finance director, another who had been a lawyer, and Janice, who managed a large call centre.

Reoffending remains a significant issue within our society. More than 24 per cent of those leaving prison return within a year, and the reasons behind this are not difficult to discern. Prisons house individuals who have failed society, yet they are often individuals who society itself has failed. A roof over their heads, someone who looks out for them, and employment upon release will significantly alter their trajectory, reducing the likelihood of returning to prison. Timpson, along with a rapidly increasing group of other employers, contributes by providing the crucial employment component.

Recruiting from prison presents several challenges, including the institutional culture focused on caring for vulnerable individuals and preventing escape. A prison is not the best place to get job ready and find the right role on release. They need help. Additionally, prison governors aren't inherently entrepreneurial, and their connections to local businesses that could employ ex-offenders are limited. Recognizing this, I persuaded a previous Secretary of State in the Justice Department, Dominic Raab, to allow me to establish Employment Advisory Boards in each of the 93 release prisons. These boards comprise of entrepreneurs leading a group of local employers, working alongside the prison governor to help connect great candidates with open-minded employers. It sounds simple, but prisons are far from straightforward.

Being an entrepreneur myself, I understand that we often deviate from standard protocols and struggle with managing intricate details. Therefore, I devised three clear goals for the boards to focus on. Firstly, I aimed to cultivate a long-term employment culture within prisons. It should be a shared objective of both inmates and staff to assist those leaving prison in finding jobs. The transient nature of prison governors, similar to that of Premier League managers, often hinders the establishment of a consistent culture across their jail. To address this, the boards aim to promote a consistent message across the prison that they are there to help people find work and reintegrate back into society over the long term. If the culture isn't there, it won't work.

Secondly, the boards focus on preparing prisoners for employment. This entails helping them create polished CVs, assisting with job applications, and arranging interviews. Although seemingly uncomplicated, these tasks can be complex within a prison environment, from opening Employment Hubs to arranging Recruitment Open Days.

Lastly, the boards aim to forge connections between prisons and local employers seeking enthusiastic and talented individuals. This enables the placement of prison leavers into full-time employment. Currently, over 90 prisons boast established boards, and the hope is that this effort will translate into a higher rate of prison leavers finding employment. Since we started in 2021, the number of people leaving prison and finding work has doubled to over 30 per cent. There is still a long way to go, but we've made a good start.

The success of these boards lies in the synergy of passionate employers, like those found at Greggs and Cook, coming together with prison staff. When top-tier businesses such as Murphy Construction and Lotus Cars champion the recruitment and support of prison leavers, they not only uplift society but also tackle their own recruitment challenges. By hiring individuals with diverse backgrounds and experiences, these companies enrich the communities in which they operate.

At Timpson, our success in recruiting and supporting ex-offenders hinges on a unique ingredient: supportive colleagues. I have initiated difficult conversations, such as 'I've met a remarkable woman in prison. She has served a lengthy sentence, lacks prior employment experience, but I believe she could excel as a cobbler. Will you take her under your wing and help her rebuild her life?' The kindness and understanding of my colleagues proved instrumental in the success of this initiative. While it might be unconventional for CEOs to publicly acknowledge employing hundreds of ex-offenders (especially if you're employing reformed burglars to cut keys), I wish more leaders would take this leap. A visit to a prison could unveil individuals who mirror themselves – ambitious, hardworking, and eager to make their families proud.

Employing ex-offenders can yield dividends far beyond the realm of business. It offers a fresh start for individuals who have faced societal failure and empowers them to rebuild their lives. It demonstrates a commitment to diversity, inclusion, and the betterment of communities. Moreover, it underscores that potential lies within every individual, regardless of their past mistakes. Timpson's approach exemplifies how recruiting the right individuals is essential for not only business success but also creating a meaningful impact on society at large. By hiring the best – those with exceptional personalities and the potential for greatness – companies pave the way for a more equitable, compassionate, and brighter future.

A TIDY WORKPLACE MEANS AN EFFICIENT TEAM

In the pursuit of building a thriving business, there's a critical factor that often goes unnoticed – the state of your surroundings. A tidy and organized workplace isn't just a superficial aspect; it's the foundation of efficiency, productivity, and customer satisfaction. Think of it as the bread and butter of your business success. The connection between pride in presentation and customer loyalty is inseparable. While it might not be the most glamorous facet of running a company, neglecting it can lead to the gradual crumbling of your business. Customers don't like to spend money with a business that doesn't care about standards.

Perfection might be elusive, but my obsession with maintaining clean and organized shops, warehouses and offices compels me to raise my voice when we falter. The sentiment I hold is clear: we might not be flawless, but cleanliness and orderliness deserve unwavering attention.

I understand the hesitance many businesses have towards investing in maintenance. It's true, new machines and exciting marketing plans tend to steal the spotlight, and reducing maintenance budgets can seem appealing, directly contributing to the bottom line, but it's a dangerous game to play. In fact, I've never known a successful business that has poor standards.

Over the past decade, identifying retail businesses on a downward spiral wasn't a complex task. A simple stroll through their shops revealed the truth – those with waning standards were often heading for a Company Voluntary Arrangement (CVA). Dingy sales floors with flickering light-bulbs, wobbly trolleys, gum-stained floors, and unkempt graphics created an unappealing shopping experience, signalling deeper issues at play. I have an untested theory. The more posters a shop has in the window the worse it's doing. When businesses are desperate for sales they flood the place with deals and special offers. These often detract from the core business and give an impression that you're desperate. In my book, clutter is as bad as litter on the floor and weeds in the car park. Instead of paying for posters in the windows, invest in spotless shops and happy colleagues.

In times of financial constraints, letting go of the cleaner might seem like a rational decision, but within my realm, cleaners are indispensable colleagues. They establish the foundation upon which all other performances are staged. My admiration extends to companies that hold high standards, with Disney taking the spotlight. To provide their guests with a 'magical experience', every cast member, from parking attendants to the CEO, takes on the role of a litter picker. A bin appears every 30 paces, toilets receive a fresh coat of paint every six weeks, and growing a beard is allowed only within the confines of a holiday break. Disney recognizes that exceptional service hinges on extraordinary standards.

At Grosvenor, the private landowner, all colleagues in their job description have 'litter picker' as a core responsibility. Wherever they are on their estates around the world, picking up litter is as important as collecting the rent. It's important that everyone in an organization is responsible for high standards.

John Robinson, a good friend of mine, manages his family's upscale jewellery business, David M Robinson. Founded by his father, David, who began his journey in Liverpool as an apprentice at the age of 15, the business is a testament to the allure of beautifully designed jewellery displayed in immaculate shops. While the company has expanded to encompass four locations, the journey hasn't been as straightforward as placing stock in the window.

Partnered with prestigious Swiss watch brands, including Rolex and Patek Philippe, the business upholds impeccable retail standards and colleague knowledge, through regular mystery shopping. Rolex, for instance, scrutinises 73 distinct observations, each a crucial component to maintaining their brand integrity and relationships. This encompasses precise display standards, and even mandates the inclusion of a hand-written thank-you letter following a sale. Maintaining such meticulous standards requires commitment, and John's dedication, along with that of his team, earns the trust of these prestigious brands.

In our own enterprise, we've developed three straightforward techniques to uphold exceptional standards. Unlike mere checklists, these techniques are rooted in a cultural approach. The journey commences with capturing photographs that exemplify a shop's best appearance. These images are showcased on a board in the stockroom, serving as a reminder that greatness is achievable. If it was pristine once, it can be so again – there's no room for ambiguity regarding how the shop should appear.

The subsequent step involves supporting colleagues when standards slip. Recognizing that maintaining a high level of appearance necessitates investment, we ensure funds are allocated towards paint, new carpets, and replacing worn shop fittings. To aid their personal presentation, we provide a 'no excuse box', equipped with two spare ties, a badge, a deodorant can, three aprons, and even a hairbrush, and razor. There should never be a reason to let standards slip.

Yet the pinnacle of our standards initiative is the eagerly anticipated 'Perfect Day'. Borrowed from Asda over a decade ago, this concept now serves as the cornerstone of our campaign to uphold high standards across our businesses. We understand that expecting unwavering perfection throughout the year might be unreasonable, but we believe that every shop, warehouse, and office can achieve perfection on a designated day annually.

The preparations for 'Perfect Day' at the office, for example, commence a month prior, as skips line up outside our office, ready to receive old documents, clutter, and outdated furniture. The buzz of excitement permeates the office on the big day, with colleagues donning their best attire – some even in black tie – to impress the judges. Points are awarded for cleanliness, and the showcasing of non-work talents. The finance team recreated a Downton Abbey scene, the buying team harmonised to 'Perfect' by Fairground Attraction, and trays of baked goods circulated in several departments to influence the judges' decisions.

Not every business will go to such lengths, and I acknowledge that our approach might appear eccentric. However, for those genuinely committed to nurturing a remarkable business, stringent standards are non-negotiable. It's no coincidence that the Navy coined the phrase, 'a clean ship is a happy ship'.

Achieving the Perfect Day: Elevating Your Business Through Exceptional Recruitment

The parallels between achieving a 'Perfect Day' in our workplace and assembling a team of remarkable individuals are both striking and profound. Just as we meticulously prepare for that special day when our surroundings shine at their best, we must adopt a discerning approach to hiring exceptional talent. If you hire the best – those 9s and 10s – achieving a 'Perfect Day' becomes not just a goal, but an attainable reality. Just as we gather our colleagues, managers, team leaders, and floor managers to create an environment of excellence, so too does this elite team contribute to our overall success. Every interaction, every engagement, every transaction hopefully becomes a symphony of perfection, resonating through the company's culture, and imprinting upon our customers' experiences. By selecting the brightest stars in the recruitment stage, we lay the foundation for our 'Perfect Day', uniting every facet of the company in a shared commitment to exceptional standards.

WHAT HAPPENS IF IT ALL GOES WRONG?

With leadership comes responsibility, and sometimes the job of the boss is to deliver bad news. No one wants to work for a company that's doing badly, letting people go, and cutting costs across the board. Someone needs to make these decisions, and someone needs to communicate them. Both these responsibilities rest on the shoulders of leaders. Part of the deal in getting paid a lot, as the boss, is that you need to be brave and you need to be good at sometimes delivering bad news.

When I first started as a head of department, I was faced with my first HR challenge. There was a colleague with a body odour problem. Everyone knew it was unacceptable, but no one wanted to raise it with them. The job rested with me, someone half their age, someone who'd never had to have that difficult conversation at work before, someone unsure of what to say. I was nervous and managed to put it off for a few weeks until I realized I'd run out of road. If I was going to be taken seriously as a leader, I had to get on with it. Running through every scenario in mind and thinking about what I was going to say, writing it down, preparing to tackle the situation head-on, I finally plucked up the courage to pop my head around the colleague's door and said that famous line, 'Can I have a word?'

The next five minutes I will never forget, because it taught me that having difficult conversations is far easier if you're honest. I said that a number of colleagues had complained to me about his body odour and that he needed to sort it out, which, if required, we would help him to do. Eventually, after we coordinated his check up, it turned out that the colleague had a medical problem that he was unaware of. So, after he'd been taken to the doctors and was prescribed some medication to take, we never had an issue in the office again.

This situation could have been handled insensitively, and a different colleague might have seen this as a reason to leave, which is not what you want when you hire people based on their incredible personalities. Instead, we managed to sort out a medical issue and improve morale in the office.

Sometimes people's behaviours are far more problematic, which means we will have to ask them to leave. It's normally because they are either in the wrong job, or they have been dishonest. Both problems require a different approach.

Sometimes we recruit a colleague and realize that they just aren't as good a fit as we hoped they'd be. We all try to make it work but sometimes you need to put your hand up and admit that we can do better. What we generally find is that if you aren't happy with someone's performance, they aren't happy either. So, we have two ways of moving on. The colleague either is given more training and time, or we part as friends. I would much prefer colleagues to be happy somewhere else than miserable with us. If these conversations are handled kindly, and with facts not emotion, we normally get a result everyone is happy with.

When we suspect someone hasn't been playing by our simple rules, and financial fair play is questioned, we have a slightly different approach. To accuse someone of theft is a big deal, so you need to make sure you're convinced, 100 per cent, that you're right. The evidence needs to support your claim, and you need to be confident that you aren't accusing someone of something that they haven't done. No one wants to go home telling their loved ones that they've been fired, so we have a big responsibility to get it right.

When it comes to the difficult conversation, we are crystal clear. This is our evidence, we believe we are right and, if we are proven right, the person under suspicion will lose their job. It's an adult conversation that no one wants to have. This is the process, but it doesn't mean you can't be kind and compassionate. Our HR team have numerous examples of colleagues that have been dismissed and subsequently contacted us to say thank you for handling it so well, and with respect for their predicament.

The easiest point in someone's career to say goodbye is when they retire. After many years of hard work it's time to hang up their hammer (as we say at Timpson), and take it easy. It's also a point in someone's career that many companies get wrong. It's a big deal and a big day for the colleague and their family, so a special celebration needs to be planned, and gifts of appreciation given. If you don't get someone's retirement right, you set a bad example to others, as it suggests long service isn't valued or respected. It should be. In our company it's a true highlight when you can say 'thank you for choosing us' to be the place for your career to thrive.

HOW TO LOOK AFTER YOUR HIGH-PERFORMING SUPER TEAM

To keep our day-to-day operations at Timpson running smoothly, while prioritizing the welfare and growth of our colleagues, we've established a comprehensive support system featuring three crucial roles: Mental Health Specialists, Financial Health First Aiders, and, most importantly, a Director of Happiness. These roles play a vital part in cultivating a thriving and united Super Team, each contributing to the over-all success and positive ambiance within the company. These roles certainly don't come cheap, but in my book it's the best money we spend.

The Mental Health Specialist

This role serves as a crucial pillar of support for the mental wellbeing of our colleagues. Trained as counsellors with expertize in mental health, they provide confidential telephone and in-person counselling to any colleague in need. They focus on problematic areas such as issues with alcohol, drugs, domestic challenges, and overall mental health. Their expert guidance helps lay the necessary foundation for overcoming addiction and mental health hurdles, ultimately contributing to a more resilient and productive Super Team. It's the least we can do to support our fantastic colleagues.

The Financial Health First Aider

In addressing financial challenges faced by our colleagues, this role takes a proactive approach to resolving monetary issues. Their dedication to assisting over 180 colleagues in the past year alone demonstrates their commitment. This expertize lies in encouraging open dialogues about an individual's financial difficulties in a safe and confidential environment. Collaboratively, they review bills, statements, and debts piling up, to develop effective plans to solve the problem once and for all. Whether through grants, company loans, connections to Credit Unions, or even aiding with bankruptcy procedures, this role equips our Super Team members with the tools to ensure their financial wellbeing for the long term.

The Director of Happiness

This distinctive role, ably carried out by Janet Leighton, revolves around providing essential support to colleagues confronting crises. Janet's empathetic approach, and willingness to provide a confidential ear, offers a lifeline to those seeking guidance. Whether organizing funerals, crafting speeches at weddings, or helping a colleague find somewhere to live, we ensure that everyone receives the vital support they need during challenging times. Going above and beyond, we even engage with external partners, as evidenced by our efforts to secure housing for colleagues with criminal records. This role embodies the caring ethos of our company and plays a pivotal part in maintaining a harmonious and supportive Super Team.

While not every organization may have the luxury of dedicated experts, the principle of prioritizing colleagues' wellbeing and nurturing their growth remains paramount. At Timpson, these roles demonstrate that every team member deserves to be heard, helped, and nurtured. By embracing the guidance of the Mental Health Specialists, the financial insights of the Financial Health First Aiders, and the compassion of the Director of Happiness, companies can foster an environment where colleagues thrive individually, and contribute collectively to a successful Super Team.

What Have We Learned?

Broaden your recruitment pool to assemble a high-performing Super Team

Embrace diversity in recruitment by considering candidates from varied backgrounds. Focus on personality traits and potential rather than just a CV. Use innovative methods like gamified psychometrics to identify exceptional talent, particularly those with personality metrics in the 9–10 range.

Empower ex-offenders

Consider hiring individuals with criminal records. Recognize their potential, dedication, and work ethic. By offering them employment, you can find very talented and hard-working people, and contribute to their rehabilitation while creating a more inclusive and diverse workforce.

Champion clean work areas

Maintain a clean and organized workplace, as it directly affects business success. Follow the examples of companies like Disney and David M Robinson, which uphold high standards for customer satisfaction and brand integrity.

Support colleague wellbeing

Establish roles dedicated to supporting colleague wellbeing. Have a Mental Health Specialist, Financial Health First Aider, and Director of Happiness to address mental health, financial challenges, and overall wellbeing. Nurture a positive and caring work environment.

Pursue excellence through recruitment

Strive for excellence by hiring the best candidates. Just as you aim for a 'Perfect Day' in terms of workplace cleanliness, select the very best talent to create a culture of high standards and exceptional performance throughout the organization, including those with personality metrics in the 9–10 range.

IF YOU BUILD IT, THEY WILL COME – HOW TO HAVE A GREAT COMPANY CULTURE

Welcome to **Lesson Two**, where we embark on a fascinating exploration of how to create an invigorating and captivating company culture that not only attracts but also retains exceptional people. In this lesson, we'll journey through the art of crafting an office environment that transcends the mundane, going far beyond the allure of now expected office perks like gyms and gourmet cafeterias.

As we delve into the realm of company culture, we'll discover that it's not merely about providing a space for people to work; it's about creating a sanctuary that embodies a company's core values. The office should be a haven, a place where colleagues can be their best selves, shielded from the struggles of daily life.

Our journey will take us back to the roots of office culture, where a childhood visit to the old Timpson head office in Wythenshawe serves as a poignant reminder that a vibrant office atmosphere should be accessible to everyone, not just high-ranking individuals. We'll explore how such an atmosphere acts as a magnetic force, enticing colleagues to eagerly step into the workplace every day.

Yet, this lesson is not merely about tangible office perks. It delves deeper into crafting an atmosphere that encapsulates a company's ethos, the very spirit that fuels its core operations. Offices should stand as secure havens, offering solace to those seeking refuge from the challenges of home life.

Moreover, investing in your office environment isn't a frivolous expense to create a facade of change; it's a strategic decision with the potential to yield significant financial returns, and sustain high retention rates. A robust company culture is a fortress guarding against stagnation, and fostering consistent growth.

Throughout this lesson, we'll encounter real-world experiences that showcase the impact of culture on a business. From the elimination of clocking-in machines, which symbolize mistrust and control, to the story of Sol, a Finnish facilities management company whose vibrant culture radiates throughout its organization, we'll gain valuable insights.

While your office location may not boast the allure of central city offices or Silicon Valley, this lesson will emphasize the importance of designing an environment that reflects and elevates your unique culture. We'll explore how even small changes, like reserving a 'Colleague of the Month' parking space, offering a free hearty breakfast, and embracing a red-carpet welcome, can have a profound impact.

And as we venture deeper into the heart of fostering an exceptional culture, we'll understand the significance of creating an apolitical and equal workplace, conducive to genuine camaraderie and self-expression.

But the essence of building a great workplace extends beyond these details. It's about making the office an enticing choice compared to endless remote meetings, all while recognizing the importance of genuine laughter as a cornerstone of success. We have a five day in-office work culture, and while this puts off some people from applying to us for a new job, it means we retain the culture we have invested in over so many years. We believe it's hard to embrace a culture if you aren't immersed within it.

Lesson Two isn't just about crafting an appealing office culture; it's about creating a nurturing environment where growth isn't just a statistic but an emotional journey, where each individual is celebrated and valued for their unique contributions.

GIVE YOUR COLLEAGUES A REASON TO GET OUT OF BED

In the world of business and office management, fostering a captivating and energizing company culture holds the key to not only attracting but retaining brilliant people. Beyond the attraction of luxury office amenities like gyms, swimming pools, and restaurants, it's the underlying culture of the company and the people that truly matters. This culture should ooze through the walls in every room.

Looking back to the roots of our office culture, I remember my childhood encounter at the old Timpson head office in Wythenshawe, a suburb of Manchester. What I realized when I thought back to that visit was that a vibrant office atmosphere isn't a luxury exclusive to those in the upper echelons of company management – it should be accessible to everyone working there, creating a magnetic pull for employees that gets them excited to come into work. Every individual in a business is equally important, and they should all be treated as such.

Investing in the office environment isn't an overindulgence in spending to make it look as if you are *trying* to change things; it's a strategic decision with the potential to yield substantial financial returns, and consistently high retention levels. A robust company culture is, perhaps, the most effective safeguard for sustained growth, and by assembling your Super Team and striving for a consistent company culture you will find that growth much easier to accomplish. I'm reminded of an experience where I was asked to advise another retailer on improving their culture. The tell-tale signs of an ailing culture were evident: unkempt surroundings, weeds and litter in the car park, little to no enthusiasm, and poor retention rates.

In our own office – known as Timpson House not Head Office – improvements have been inspired by other successful companies I've visited with strong cultures. One of the best companies that I have seen with a robust culture that spreads throughout the entire business is Sol, a Finnish facilities management company. The ordinary exterior of their office building in Helsinki housed an interior bursting with vibrancy and joy, anchored by the owner's love for the colour yellow.

Although our location in Wythenshawe might lack the allure of city centre offices or Silicon Valley, we've concentrated on designing an environment that both represents and elevates our culture. Small changes can wield substantial impact. Our car park boasts no reserved spots for executives, except for the 'Colleague of the Month' space that is reserved for the highest-performing team member of that month. A free hearty breakfast greets early arrivals, our receptionists are known throughout the company as our Directors of Smiles, and a red carpet leads the way into the building, acknowledging each and every one of our Very Important Colleagues as they begin their days.

A simple yet profound sign at reception – 'Please leave your politics in the car park' – emphasizes the significance of nurturing an apolitical workplace, where genuine camaraderie and self-expression can thrive.

Another old fashioned and unnecessary feature of a traditional office is the clocking in machine. For me, the concept of clocking-in embodies mistrust and management control, signalling a need for an introspective evaluation of recruitment practices. So we don't use them. Exceptional colleagues – like the ones that you will be hiring – don't require surveillance to perform, and aren't driven by being in on time; they thrive within an inspiring culture where they are trusted.

The overall aim of building a great place of work is to make the office a more alluring option compared to endless Zoom calls, while emphasizing the importance of genuine laughter. My belief is rooted in the notion that the more laughter that resonates throughout the office, the more prosperous our shops become. Of course, there are times when businesses will need to work across multiple locations and will have to employ measures to accommodate those working from home. However, if you build it they will come. We have a five-day-a-week culture in the office, and we don't get push-back on this. Because it's a fun place to work, colleagues are prepared to battle with the traffic to get in on time ... five days a week. Having an office environment that is attractive throughout the year is a massive pull for everyone working with us and by giving back, consistently and without discrimination or favouritism, is a guaranteed way to make sure everyone is happy coming into work.

WANT MORE STAFF IN THE OFFICE? GIVE THEM EXTRA DAYS OFF

Among the many complex business theories that leaders aim to follow, there is one unconventional idea that stands out for me, defying established finance norms, untouched by an academic's approval and causing even the most composed human resources managers to shift in their seats. It's a notion that might raise an eyebrow: offering *additional* paid days off to colleagues celebrating significant life moments as a driver of business success and employee happiness. While this might seem like a theory that is counterintuitive, especially when considering the resources needed to successfully complete a day's duties, it's the best money you can spend. Pay is not enough to create loyalty, but kindness and recognition of an individual's life does. The more days off we give, the better we seem to do.

The environment in which we work needs to appeal to our emotions just as much as it appeals to our career and financial ambitions. It needs to be accessible to everyone, where there are no favourites. At Oracle's head office in San Francisco, the founder Larry Ellison has his own lift. In our book the offices are designed so everyone has the same desk, chair, and PC, and everyone can use the lift! It's the same when it comes to days off. It's for everyone, not just the bosses.

The foundation of this philosophy often rests upon the empathy and wisdom of a finance director who understands the art of balancing the books and nurturing the human spirit. A remarkable figure, like Paresh Majithia, who stepped into the world of Timpson 21 years ago as Finance Director, and embraced a whirlwind of unconventional work practices, which required a leap of faith that seldom finds a place in the rigid frameworks of finance. They certainly don't teach you this in accountancy school.

Through friendships like that of Richard and Dawn O'Sullivan, who lead a chain of juice bars called Boost, came a spark that ignited a transformative approach: the concept of additional days off to celebrate birthdays, enjoy cherished family moments, or simply recover from a night of celebration. The brilliance lay in its simplicity and kindness, even though it entailed a cost.

Over time, the 'birthday off' transformed into a cornerstone of the employment experience at Timpson. In a world where there are lots of potential employees and employers, the idea of an extra day off for your own birthday has an undeniable pull.

The strategy grew from strength to strength, celebrating life's pivotal moments with extended time off. Weddings were the next big days to tackle: each person is given an additional paid week off, £100 towards the flowers, and even a chauffeur-driven car for the big day. If it happens to be a wedding between co-workers, we double the amount. This is an approach that might raise the eyebrows of some finance directors but one that confirms the commitment of the company to the people behind the operations.

Birthdays and weddings were a given once we started on this path, but now other monumental moments in colleagues' personal lives were embraced. When an employee fretted over missing her daughter's first day of school due to no longer having any annual leave available, the solution was crystal clear: an extra day off for each colleague when their children started school. Being there to wave them off at the school gates is an experience no parent should miss.

The journey didn't stop there. The spectrum of experiences that deserve recognition has expanded to include all manner of extra days, including a 'pet bereavement day' and 'Grandparents' Day', a testament to Timpson's commitment to family values and the myriad emotions that define our lives.

With these additional days off, a unique culture takes root, resonating with the team and setting the business apart. While the immediate financial gains might not be apparent, the dividends of an emotionally invested workforce extend beyond the bottom line, shaping a workplace where every individual is seen, celebrated, and valued for all their contributions. This isn't merely a tale of time off; it's a long-standing story of appreciation, empathy, and a belief that by giving back, businesses can build a legacy and culture that transcends profit margins.

WHAT IF SOMETHING GOES WRONG?

Inflation is rising, and businesses are grappling with soaring costs and government-imposed complexity. While tough decisions may be necessary at times, one critical aspect that should remain non-negotiable is paying your colleagues and team members fairly. This commitment to fair compensation not only demonstrates your support for them but also plays a vital role in retaining valuable talent during challenging times.

The current economic landscape is drastically different from what it was before worldwide disruptions, such as Covid, the cost of living crisis, and Brexit. What were once manageable ripples now feel like a tsunami. Wage inflation has reared its head, import prices have skyrocketed, and government taxes are becoming even more onerous. It's imperative that businesses promptly reassess their operational models to adapt to these unprecedented global factors.

Reflecting on history, we can look back to the inflation crisis of 1975 when prices surged nearly 27 per cent, and the economic crash of 2007–08, which had far-reaching consequences. In response to the 1975 crisis, the Government limited salary increases, leading businesses to raise prices repeatedly to survive, often four times in a year.

In this challenging environment, retaining and recruiting top talent is paramount. While the temptation to hastily fill vacancies may arise, it's essential to maintain high standards in hiring and ensure that the company culture is consistent, despite external factors. Exceptional colleagues want to work alongside equally outstanding peers, making it crucial for businesses to maintain this delicate balance.

Our strategy to navigate these challenges comprises two steps. First, we continue to award significant pay increases for every member of our company, along with additional increments during their next personal pay review. While this may not impact the overall inflation rate, it will enhance our ability to attract and retain exceptional employees.

Businesses that prioritize fair compensation, colleague well-being, and fostering a culture of kindness will not only endure, but will also thrive in the face of the storms we currently sail into. Just as rough seas forge stronger sailors, companies that pay well and support their people will emerge stronger from these turbulent times.

Our colleagues don't merely wear a uniform; they embody our culture.

DON'T GET BOGGED DOWN IN THE DATA: SIMPLICITY IS KEY

These days, technology allows us to gather an unprecedented amount of information. One might assume that the more data we have, the better our decisions will be. However, I have a confession to make . . . I barely ever read any of the data that our business produces. That might sound unconventional in an era where data analytics and insights are highly prized, but at Timpson we have always taken a different approach – one that revolves around the simplicity of traditional methods, autonomy and focus.

In March of 2020, when the shops closed, and our colleagues were on furlough, there wasn't much data to analyse. While that might have caused sleepless nights for some leaders, I couldn't help but wonder if having more data would have made the situation any clearer at all. We didn't know there was going to be a global pandemic so it seems ironic to me that the modern business world places such an immense emphasis on data, while we place our focus on the people. Often, I am asked whether we think this puts us behind the time in certain respects, but I don't quite think it does.

While new forms of data have undoubtedly brought about revolutionary ideas and trends, there is a point where data can cease to be useful when we become overly reliant on it. If we look at Billy Beane, famously portrayed by Brad Pitt in *Moneyball*, for instance, we can see that data could significantly impact decision-making in base-ball, helping his team win against the odds. But can that same data-driven approach be applied to a shoe repair business? I doubt it.

With all our shops open again and everyone back in the office, the data is pouring in once again. With over 2,000 shops, numbers and details flow in from every department at an alarming rate. However, we've intentionally built a culture at Timpson that advocates producing as little information as possible, because in the end, it's not about drowning in data but instead, focusing on what truly matters.

Our business philosophy revolves around answering two key questions:

1. Are the shops open?
2. Is everyone happy?

If the answers to these two questions are a resounding yes, then we can get down to business – taking in money, satisfying our customers, and ensuring everyone's wellbeing is looked after. These simple questions are at the heart of our strategy and keep us grounded in our approach.

Our first barometer for success is when the sales data we receive each night at 7pm arrives. What's unique about this data is that it isn't collected by a high-tech Electronic Point of Sale (EPOS) till system. Instead, our colleagues take five minutes at the end of each day to fill out an online form and write down the sales numbers on a piece of paper, which they keep on a bulldog clip. This might seem old-fashioned, but it works wonders. There's a connection between the act of physically writing things down and taking more notice of them. Our colleagues know their daily sales figures within a

£50 margin because they've personally recorded them that day.

In contrast to our approach, some of the businesses we've acquired over the years have relied heavily on EPOS tills and the collection of an abundance of data. However, most of this data went unused and did little to improve customer service. As sales began to plummet, and as more data was analyzed, financial experts and consultants were brought in to uncover the root of the issues. Unfortunately, it was the front-line team, the ones dedicated to serving customers, who more often than not were going to be the people to lose their jobs first. This data overload can take some companies away from what is truly important – providing exceptional customer service.

Our second barometer is our customer service scores, which I personally review each day. We simply ask our customers to rate their experience using an online form on a scale of 1–10 (our average is 9.2). Every colleague can see their feedback in real-time, and if we receive a low score, our Area Managers are tasked with contacting the dissatisfied customer, apologizing and resolving the issue. In this context, one piece of data trumps all others.

Finally, there's one ultimate marker that surpasses all others – the health of our business. This was a lesson my father imparted to me 25 years ago. He told me that the best way to measure the health of a business is by examining the cash figure every day. Each morning, around 10 a.m., I receive an email from someone in our finance team, detailing the amount of cash we have in the bank compared to the same date last year. These figures leave no room for interpretation or evasion.

The year-on-year comparison is the truest measure of our cash flow's strength and an indicator of whether we are genuinely profitable.

While modern reporting methods and data analytics have their roles to play, focusing on cash is our anchor. It's astonishing how many senior executives I meet who have no idea about their company's cash position. Concentrating on our bank balance proved invaluable when the pandemic hit. When you're losing a million pounds a week, budgets and strategic plans go out the window. However, when you thoroughly understand your cash flow, you're better equipped to weather the storm and gain the trust of the banks.

In all aspects of our business, we focus on simplicity. Of course, there are times when data is necessary – such as the customer feedback reports and our internal Happy Index – but only if it leads to better decision-making and eliminates the need to generate even more reports, that then take away valuable resources to produce something that no one reads. One thing I will stand firm on though is my unwavering commitment to keeping an eagle eye on our cash flow. It's the key to a good night's sleep and the ultimate measure of any company's health.

At Timpson, we developed the Happy Index so that it serves as an essential part of our business culture. This index focuses on the questions that truly matter, reflecting our commitment to the people we work with. The simplicity of the Happy Index is a reflection of our core beliefs, and acts as a guide for our leaders, teams, and colleagues. It is an uncomplicated yet effective way to measure and enhance our colleagues' job satisfaction, and by using the same simplicity in our customer feedback we know that the data is easy to understand, based on fact, and gives us the ability to quickly rectify any issues for dissatisfied customers (of which there aren't very many). Happy customers means repeat business, and making sure that you're on top of this is crucial, especially if you work in the customer-facing retail industry. You need to be across this key facet.

Simply put, below are the pieces of data that you need to know about – the rest will be ably handled by the Super Team you've brought together.

Daily sales data

By keeping track of our sales figures and writing them down with pen and paper at the end of each day, your colleagues will know exactly what to do, and you can rest assured it is being handled.

Customer service scores

In continuously assessing our customer service quality via online feedback forms, we can address and improve on parts of the business that need resolving swiftly and effectively. If you don't work with 'customers', think about the suppliers, freelancers, project managers, and clients you serve. Are you doing the best for them, and have you asked?

Cash flow analysis

Cash flow is at the core of any business. Make sure to rigorously evaluate your daily cash position compared to the same day the previous year, to make sure you're working towards a profitable year.

Our surveys, along with the straightforward questions, and our commitment to simplicity and tradition, give us the tools to create an overall sense of happiness, from the customer and shop manager to the receptionist and the finance manager. By maintaining clarity in communication, and allowing everyone to work with autonomy, you can create an environment where everyone works together toward the shared goal of making profit, while ensuring that everyone is content and thriving in their roles within the business.

Established, simple, and trusted approaches allow for everyone to concentrate on the most crucial aspect of their role, which is much more important than reading another set of numbers.

Some Easy Wins for Building a Great Company Culture

Designing a captivating environment
Create an office environment that mirrors your company's values and offers a haven for employees.

Prioritizing culture over amenities
While amenities matter, focus on instilling a robust culture that resonates with your team. You can't have one without the other.

Cultivating trust, not control
Replace clocking-in machines with a culture of trust and inspiration.

Learning from others
Borrow ideas from successful companies to enhance your office atmosphere; it doesn't have to cost a fortune.

Fostering a laughter-filled workplace
Cultivate an atmosphere of genuine laughter, as it correlates with business success.

Ultimately, there are unlimited ways in which you can ensure that your company has a clear, individual culture, built around the day-to-day needs of both the business as a whole, and its employees. The more time and effort you invest in this area, the better the business will perform.

HOW WELL DO YOU KNOW YOUR TEAM?

As with a lot of things here at Timpson, we like to make sure that everyone is able to work collaboratively on a daily basis, whether that be in their exchanges with colleagues working on the shopfloor or in the warehouse, the people they encounter in other areas of the business or in meetings and, of course, the wider support team.

To make sure that everyone feels comfortable, there is no talk of differing political opinions, as that is not suitable talk for the workplace, and could lead to unnecessary disagreements based on others' thoughts and beliefs. However, what we do ask people to do, especially when they are in a management role, is to take a little test to see how they score when asked a few simple, personal questions about their colleagues, the answers to which should be easy in any successful business relationship.

Companies all too often forget that the people they are working alongside are the most valued asset to their business. I've said it once and I will say it again, the happiness of your colleagues is an easy win to achieve financial targets. It starts with people getting to know your personality and skills in the workplace but is further strengthened by the entire team getting to know a bit more about your personal life and hobbies outside of work. No, it doesn't mean that they should know your address and where you're going to be on Friday night but having an appreciation of your colleagues' interests allows for the entire team to fully appreciate the drivers behind an individual's success.

Using the questionnaire on the next page, select a member of your team and populate this with your answers as best you can.

Do you know your people?

SUBJECT (add the name of your chosen colleague here)

1. What is their partner's name? (10 points)

2. Where did they last go on holiday? (10 points)

3. Do they have any pets and what are their names? (10 points)

4. What are their hobbies? (5 points)

5. What would they like for their birthday for £20 or less? (5 points)

6. What do they drink? (5 points)

7. What car do they drive? (5 points)

8. What sports team do they support? (5 points)

9. What are the names and ages of their children? (20 points)

10. Where is home? (5 points)

11. Favourite TV show? (10 points)

12. What's their music taste? (5 points)

13. Best idea of a night out (e.g. clubbing, cinema, night in, pub)? (5 points)

Now that you've filled this out, go and double-check the answers with your colleague.

If you've achieved more than 70 points you are a certified 'people person' and know the people that you work with very well.

If you've scored less than 70 points, it might be time to ask your colleague a bit more about themselves. Why don't you try inviting them for a coffee, or going out for lunch one day, and getting to understand their personal life a bit more?

The above exercise isn't intended to make anyone feel that they don't know their colleague, but instead is used to highlight areas for improvement. It also encourages everyone to get to know one another, so that there are no issues further on down the line.

COMPANY CULTURE IS ALSO CUSTOMER CULTURE

When I'm out visiting branches, which I do two to three days a week, I check in with every member of the team to ask them how they are, and to make sure business is going smoothly. On one occasion, a colleague had been subjected to verbal abuse from a customer, reducing them to tears and leaving them concerned for their safety. In a situation that was not their fault, a customer had wrongly accused them of an error, unleashing a barrage of offensive, sexist language, accompanied by intimidating gestures. Sometimes the customer isn't right.

Regrettably, this isn't an isolated incident, and I don't imagine it will be the last time I hear reports of this going on. It's a growing problem affecting millions of people who work in customer service, striving to do their best, earn a living, and support their families. This behaviour is completely unacceptable and has become a source of mounting concern for many business leaders.

However, what sets us apart at Timpson is our deep-rooted commitment to a unique company culture that transcends our team and extends to the treatment of our staff in branches. Our culture is one founded on principles of respect, kindness, and understanding. It's a culture that has proven not only to be the cornerstone of our success but also a driving force behind our compassionate approach to customer interactions.

Our colleagues don't merely wear a uniform; they embody our culture. When a customer walks into a Timpson store, they don't just encounter a salesperson; they meet someone who is a product of our inclusive and empathetic work environment, which fosters an atmosphere of mutual respect and appreciation. For many of our colleagues, welcoming a customer into their shop has the same importance as welcoming them into their home.

We've seen the transformative power of treating colleagues with kindness and respect, which then extends to how our teams interact with customers. It's a virtuous cycle that can make our shops, and indeed all places of customer service, better for everyone involved.

In a report published by the British Retail Consortium, incidents of abuse directed at shop staff have surged to over 450 per day. The Institute of Customer Service reports that over half of workers in the retail, hospitality, and transport sectors have faced abuse while at work. Unlike soldiers who expect to face challenges when they enlist, individuals applying for jobs behind a shop counter don't anticipate encountering such hostility.

In addition to retail, the medical field has its share of similar stories. A friend of mine who is a GP has recounted various instances where patients have used foul and abusive language at his surgery, particularly when they couldn't secure their preferred appointment time or receive their prescription instantly. In hospital emergency rooms, the situation can be even worse, with some patients believing that raising their voice and causing a scene will expedite their own care or that of a loved one, at the expense of others.

Teachers are no strangers to this issue either, as they often face difficulties not solely from the children they educate, but from the parents of those children. Inappropriate verbal abuse, criticism, and relentless contact through social media and emails have even coined the term 'parent bombing'. While parental involvement is essential for students' progress, it should always be respectful and proportionate.

Our company culture is a testament to the fact that creating a positive work environment should lead to a more respectful and understanding customer base. It's about treating everyone with decency and valuing each other's contributions. My instinct is to believe my colleagues are right and have made a decision in good faith, despite the pressure they are sometimes faced with.

Those individuals on the front line work hard to provide excellent service, and they deserve appreciation and empathy from customers who recognize the challenges they face. Let the influence of our culture at Timpson remind us all of the power of respect, kindness, and understanding in creating a better world, both inside and outside our stores.

INVEST IN TRAINING COLLEAGUES TO ENSURE COMPANY CULTURE IS RETAINED

Early in my career, I had a profound encounter that forever changed my perspective on the value of training and investing in employees. I visited the family of a colleague named Brian, who had tragically passed away in his early forties. As I entered their home, the walls were adorned with certificates showcasing Brian's career achievements within our company. His pride in those accomplishments was evident, and it extended to his family. That moment left an indelible mark on me, highlighting the significance of training and professional growth, not just for individuals but for their families and communities as well.

At Timpson, we've always understood the paramount importance of nurturing our colleagues' talents and potential. While the shoe repair trade is a unique blend of craftsmanship and retail, we've consistently prioritized our own training programs over generic retail schemes. We firmly believe that investing in our people is not only a matter of financial investment but also a reflection of our core values.

Our commitment to colleague training revolves around two primary areas. First, we have our well-established apprenticeship scheme, which covers the practical skills essential for the job. This scheme has remained virtually unchanged for over two decades, offering a comprehensive 16-week program encompassing topics like health and safety, customer care, key cutting, and even engraving pet tags. In our eyes, qualifications earned through this program are not just badges of expertize; they are directly linked to pay raises and promotional opportunities. The more our colleagues learn, the more they earn. This core principle underscores our dedication to recognizing and rewarding talent within our ranks.

However, our commitment to training extends far beyond practical skills. In recognition of the fact that effective leadership and interpersonal competencies are equally crucial in our business, my dad John led the development of a range of courses tailored to these soft skills. These courses, much like this book, include 'how to recruit for personality', 'how to have difficult conversations' and 'how to be a caring boss'. We firmly believe that having a well-rounded skill set is imperative for our colleagues, as they play an essential role in running our business.

But it's not just about training within our own industry; it's about instilling our ethos in every aspect of our colleagues' lives. We understand that a skilled and motivated workforce is a tremendous asset. However, the training landscape in the UK has often been more of a hindrance than a help, bogged down by bureaucracy and inefficient training providers that delay progression.

The Apprenticeship Levy, introduced in 2015, was initially a beacon of hope, offering a new way for streamlining our training budget. Unfortunately, our in-house apprenticeship scheme, which stands as the most comprehensive in our industry, did not align with the Levy's guidelines, leading to substantial expenses that could not be recouped. We basically didn't tick enough boxes.

Despite the financial challenges posed by the Levy, we remain committed to nurturing the potential of our colleagues and helping them thrive. We've found creative ways to make use of the funds we contribute. Currently, 25 per cent of our unspent Levy funds are redirected toward supporting apprenticeships in nursing and social care through the Essex Apprenticeship Levy transfer service. This initiative aligns with our ethos of giving back to the community and promoting personal growth (something I will go on to discuss in **Lesson Five**).

However, many of the Levy's restrictions do not align with our unique training approach. For example, the requirement that 20 per cent of the course must be off-site and that apprenticeships must last a minimum of 12 months does not suit our needs. We know the best way to train our recruits, given our industry-specific expertize, and it is near impossible for those not within the industry to train colleagues in all aspects of the company's ethos.

To further underscore our commitment to training, we've established the Timpson UniverCity, our purpose-built £4 million NEST training centre in Manchester. Here, our ambitious colleagues can enrol in a degree course focusing on Upside-Down Management, our distinctive approach to running the company. At the NEST we never talk about the technical skills needed to serve our customers, we instead concentrate on how we nurture our culture, and care for our colleagues. We hope one day to welcome non-Timpson colleagues on to our courses, and maybe raise some money for our Foundation along the way.

In conclusion, our investment in colleague training is a testament to our core values. We believe in hiring the best, treating them well, and retaining them by unlocking their potential. While the Apprenticeship Levy has presented its own set of challenges, we continue to explore innovative ways to foster growth and skill development within our workforce. For us, training is not just about certificates and qualifications; it's about empowering our colleagues to become the best they can be, both within our company and in their broader lives.

Parkinson's Law

In my early twenties, my dad gifted me a collection of essays, one of which I found truly insightful and refer back to regularly, even to this day. 'Parkinson's Law', an essay written for the *Economist* by C Northcote Parkinson explained his thinking behind 'work expands to fill the time available for its completion'.

Simply put, if you have 10 days to complete a task, it will take you 10 days to get it done; if you give yourself 5 days for the same task, you'll manage to finish it in 5 days. Inadequate deadlines often cause procrastination and spending too much time on trivial matters.

Imagine Sarah working diligently on a project in a modern office setting, feeling overwhelmed by the workload. Recognizing the need for assistance, she decides to expand her team because she feels over worked. While initially a one-person team, she understands that with more hands on deck, the project's efficiency and productivity can significantly improve. Sarah recruits two colleagues, John and Emily, to join her project. Her rationale is that by bringing in skilled individuals, they can divide the tasks, leading to a more balanced workload and quicker project completion. It also means Sarah gets a pay rise for taking on more responsibility.

However, as John and Emily join the team, they complete their assigned tasks efficiently and actively seek additional responsibilities to stay productive. This proactive approach unintentionally results in a more complex workload. Although the team has grown from one to three members, it hasn't necessarily increased overall productivity.

This scenario illustrates Parkinson's Law, where the expansion of a team can sometimes lead to unexpected complexities and inefficiencies. At Timpson, we recognize the significance of hiring skilled individuals tailored to specific functions. While team expansion can be beneficial, it must be carefully managed to ensure it aligns with our ethos of hiring the best and treating them well while enhancing overall productivity. It's ok to say yes to good ideas that may help the business, but if they increase costs, headcount, and complexity, I tend to give them a wide berth.

EMPLOYEE WELLNESS

When I started in our business over 25 years ago, you still could smoke in the office, and many of the people working for the company would tootle off to the burger van that sat at the end of the road for regular snacks and meals throughout the day. If it wasn't a cigarette or a burger, you might find some members of the team heading to the pub for a couple of pints over a liquid lunch. This wasn't unique to Timpson nor the retail industry, it was typical of most businesses at the time. There was a big change in 1996 when we introduced an office smoking ban, although some colleagues protested, so this was paused every lunchtime when the whole office then filled with smoke again!

Fortunately, times have changed since then and people seeking jobs tend to recognize that a key part of an employer's brand, as well as their commitment to company culture, is the encouragement of a healthier workforce – physically and mentally – to ensure that their wellbeing is looked after when they join the company. At Timpson, this comes down to a few key things that we've already discussed: a dedicated member of the team who looks after individuals' mental health, and a company culture that supports people in all avenues of their life, including making better, healthier choices. We no longer have vending machines full of quick snacks and there's no burger van lurking outside the doors. In fact, I've banned them from coming to our office at all in favour of other, more health-conscious initiatives.

But is it a company's job to show colleagues the path to a healthier lifestyle, or should it just be left to the state and the individual?

To me, this is simple. If your team are healthy, and we help to support that through in-house wellbeing programmes, we find that there is a significant reduction in colleague absences as, largely, everyone is fit for work. Of course, if there's a problem, there are also ways for us to work around that to support the person in need. So, no, the health of your colleagues should not be left solely to state-funded initiatives but should work in combination to protect the needs of the business and ensure that your most vital commodity – those you work with – are able to happily and safely come into work.

In 2014, Harvard Business School published a report that explained how US companies are able to save $3.27 for every $1 spent on company-driven wellness programmes, further evidence that investing in your colleagues not only helps them but also saves money in the long run.

While all of this sounds sensible, and if a few moving parts were able to be put in place, it could work more widely, this change also needs to be done alongside any other commercial challenges that you may face daily. Overall, people decide to join companies to develop their careers and better their livelihoods, not because they've got the latest line up of gym equipment.

In January, many gym operators' marketing teams go into overdrive, pulling out all the stops to sign up new customers who start the New Year with resolutions that are focused on their health and fitness. While the number of gym fans may dwindle as their initial enthusiasm wears off, corporate membership schemes produce a much higher level of retention. However, when the world found itself facing repeated lockdowns, and nobody could access their local gym, Joe Wicks was able to get the UK moving with over a million people tuning in on a regular basis to watch him live each morning. That daily exercise, and the new world we have found ourselves in, since the pandemic has generally led people to pursue a healthier balance in their life, which is important for employers to appreciate. One of the biggest growth areas on our high streets is shops offering healthier, less processed food.

Scott Best, a director at Fitness First, reported that the company successfully retained over 95 per cent of their corporate clients during the pandemic, and 15 per cent of their January joiners were likely to be corporate clients. These are typically salary-sacrifice schemes, wherein the company contributes or matches the amount from their colleagues' salaries to allow them to benefit from a gym membership while in their employment.

Alongside salary-sacrifice schemes like those for a gym membership, other companies also offer colleagues free subscriptions to wellbeing services and apps, such as Headspace and Calm; rewards for walking or cycling to and from work; access to a mental health specialist available 24 hours a day; private healthcare; free eye examinations; maternity care support; and many, many more. These are all positive steps in the right direction to not only attracting and retaining the very best people, but also fostering a company culture of support and understanding.

One hugely important promise is our commitment to allowing time off and paying for any prescription medication for the women in our company that need additional support due to the menopause (see page 98). I believe this should absolutely be a key part of every company's promise – to support their colleagues' needs and allow them to do the best in their job.

A Company Gym Isn't for Everyone

Now, I know I said earlier that having an office gym isn't going to solve all your problems, but we have one as part of our employer offer, and it's a wise investment, even if you're adding a few weights and a treadmill. Even if we ran out of office space in the future, we would never downsize the gym.

When we redesigned the offices, more than a decade ago now, we had some spare space that wasn't needed, and decided that the most economical way to fill that space and give people opportunities to take themselves away from the working day while on their break, was to put in a few bits of gym equipment. Then I got carried away . . .

To understand how the office fitness area should be set up, I tracked down a few companies that had great colleague-only gyms and asked if I could take a peek at their in-house areas. Naturally, my competitiveness kicked in and I wanted to have the best on-site gym of any other company. So, what was supposed to be a small area for those wanting to carve out some time and get a quick gym session in by using one of the exercise bikes, free weights, or running machine, quickly turned into a full-on health and lifestyle gym, with showers, a swimming pool, and even a sauna.

Initially, enthusiasm for the new area was nuts, and the number of colleagues who wanted to use the facilities meant that we needed to create a booking sheet. To get around the number of people wishing to attend, we started keeping the office open from 6am to 8pm to cope with demand. When interviewing prospective candidates as part of the 'sell', our gym was one of the main attractions during the office tour. Being a member of our own gym meant that you didn't have to pay an annual membership to join one of your own, so it was seen as an attractive financial benefit to prospective new members of the team.

Quickly, though, numbers reduced.

However, despite the drop in numbers, there was a group of hardcore fitness fanatics who continued to attend. The next step was to recruit 'Fitness Chris' as the company trainer. Chris is still with us to this day, focused on delivering early morning boot camps and after-work circuit training. Alongside the running club and five-a-side football team, the gym is still a benefit that many of the team greatly enjoy, despite it not being for everyone.

If you're looking to add additional benefits to your company's package that support your colleagues and their health, I'd look to the very simple solution of setting up deals with local gyms which give discounted membership, but also access to exercise classes, such as yoga and Pilates.

The most used lifestyle benefit we have on offer at our offices is very simple: free fruit. We have bowls planted around the offices, full of apples, pears, and bananas, which colleagues are free to take as much as they would like to. As with my attempt at setting up a gym for staff to use, when the scheme was initially introduced we went through more boxes of fruit than Chester Zoo use to feed their animals. Fortunately, it's calmed down now. When the free-fruit initiative was first up and running, our average bill for the fruit at the end of each fiscal year was over £10,000. While this may cover part of the costs in advertising, hiring and training a new starter, it's one of our most important benefits, and the positives far outweigh the negative associations with the cost, as we are prioritizing our colleagues' health. (These days, with rising costs, the spend has topped out at £17,000 per year, which equates to around 40,000 pieces of fruit each year!)

There are many ways you can offer help to the team in supporting their physical and mental health. I understand that not everyone has the financial capabilities to build a custom gym in their offices, but showing that you are willing to make steps is a way to keep everyone motivated and feel that you care. It costs nothing to set up a running club.

What Have We Learned?

Prioritize employee health

In **Lesson Two**, we've delved into the critical aspects of prioritizing employee wellbeing and health, recognizing their immense value in fostering a productive and content workforce. It all begins with putting the health of your employees at the forefront, encouraging a culture that values both physical and mental health. Understand that this is a joint responsibility, with company and state-funded initiatives working in partnership to ensure a fit and effective workforce. By prioritizing health, you not only support your colleagues but also safeguard the operational needs of your business.

Invest in wellbeing programs

Consider making investments in employee wellbeing programs. These initiatives often prove to be cost-effective in the long run. Provide benefits such as gym memberships and free subscriptions to wellbeing services and apps. These steps demonstrate your commitment to supporting employee mental health and overall wellbeing, contributing to a more satisfied and engaged team.

Small gestures matter

Sometimes, it's the little things that make a significant difference. Initiatives like offering free fruit can have a profound impact on employee health and morale. Even if setting up a fully-equipped gym in your offices isn't feasible, these small steps can keep everyone motivated and healthy. If you offer to pay for colleagues' prescriptions, provide them with support in their personal lives or make adjustments to their office days, you send a strong message to a cohort that often feels left out and misunderstood.

Leverage corporate memberships

Corporate membership schemes for gyms or fitness facilities can be a game-changer. They not only promote physical health but also encourage a healthier work-life balance among employees. Such schemes often result in higher retention rates compared to individual memberships, making them a valuable addition to your wellbeing offerings.

Support balance in life

Foster a company culture that genuinely values and supports a healthy work-life balance. Understand that it's not just about work; it's about nurturing a holistic approach to life that includes physical and mental health, making for happier and more productive employees.

TO GET AHEAD, YOU'VE GOT TO GET ABOUT

Welcome to **Lesson Three**, where we will delve into the essential aspects of achieving lasting success in business. In this chapter, we'll explore the dynamic world of Timpson and its unique approach to thriving in a competitive landscape. As the CEO of Timpson, I'll take you on a journey through the principles that have allowed our company to not only succeed but also continuously evolve and excel.

In the ever-changing business landscape, staying ahead of the curve is paramount. To do so, it's essential to be aware of the competition and draw inspiration from successful companies. At Timpson, we've made it a habit to study our rivals and learn from their achievements. It's not about copying them, but rather understanding what works and incorporating those insights into our day-to-day operations.

By keeping a close eye on industry leaders and emerging trends, we gain valuable perspectives that inform our strategic decisions. The key here is adaptability. Successful businesses are those that can pivot and embrace change while staying true to their core values.

Learning from the best

In the world of business, there's an adage that goes, 'It's not about reinventing the wheel, but rather making it better'. This philosophy resonates deeply at Timpson. We understand that to thrive in a competitive market, it's vital to learn from the successes and failures of others.

For instance, when it comes to customer service, we look to companies like Apple and Amazon. These giants have redefined customer expectations, and their customer-centric approach has inspired us to continuously improve our own service. We've adapted their principles to fit our unique business model, ensuring that our customers receive exceptional service at every Timpson location.

Adaptability in action

One of the most remarkable aspects of successful companies is their ability to adapt to changing circumstances. The business landscape is constantly evolving, and those who can't adjust are at risk of being left behind.

For example, during the Covid pandemic, we saw an unprecedented shift in consumer behaviour. People relied more on online shopping, and foot traffic in our high street stores dwindled. In response, we quickly pivoted to expand our online presence and offer new services to meet changing customer needs. Our adaptability allowed us to not only survive but thrive in challenging times.

THE HAPPY INDEX

Businesses love measuring things. Whether it's going well or badly, finance teams produce reams of data that paint a picture of what's going on. Management schools often refer to Peter Drucker's saying that 'you can't manage what you can't measure'. It's straightforward to measure sales, profits, and balance sheets, but how easy is it to measure the most important barometer in any business: *how happy are your colleagues?*

The way colleagues feel reflects the way our customers will feel. If we get it right customers will enjoy the experience of shopping with us and return. We see this clearly through our sales figures. The colleagues that are the happiest consistently bring in the best sales.

This is why we look for ways to measure happiness, and it has become the focus of the way we run the business. Colleagues' happiness comes before anything else. Most companies have annual employee satisfaction surveys, and I've seen the good and the bad, including some that are ridiculously long, often with pointless questions to answer. I sense that these are put in to provide answers to satisfy an internal political problem, or at the whim of a disgruntled colleague. Only last week I saw a survey that included the questions, 'Do you feel you're paid a fair wage for how hard you work?' and 'Would working from home on a Friday improve your work-life balance?' You can guess what the majority of answers will be.

At Timpson, we do our surveys differently by asking just one question: 'On a scale of 1 to 10 how happy are you with the support you get from your team?' Alongside this numerical metric, we also leave a space for additional comments so that we can get a complete response to identify any areas in the business that are working well for everyone or, as with every company, those parts that could be slightly improved to make our colleagues' jobs that bit easier. Our response rate in 2019 was 84 per cent, while most other company surveys average less than 30 per cent, and our figure increased to 86 per cent in

2023. The high response rate is, perhaps, due to the simplicity of our survey.

In 2020, at the height of Covid, the survey went out to our 4,000 colleagues, and for the first time in a long time I was concerned about what the results would be, as we took some drastic measures due to national lockdowns and went into survival mode. During this time, we made colleagues redundant, closed eighteen shops, and stopped some of our most popular colleague benefits. However, while there certainly are some scars from this time, we did help foster a supportive work environment, which was proved by the successful Happy Index scores (an overall average score of 9.1/10 in 2023, which differs to the 8.6/10 average before Covid).

Like most companies, we had some difficult days during Covid and, at times, were operating on the wrong side of panic. I believe the best place to be as a company is just on the right side of panic. Everyone understands that at times we go into overdrive when a new initiative kicks in or an acquisition is made, but it shouldn't last long because it makes everyone unhappy. Covid led us to be on the wrong side of panic for far too long. While some businesses can operate their organisations successfully in the short term by being reactive, it does not allow for thoughtful leadership. If it goes on too long, the engine overheats and you start dropping things that you would typically manage well in your day-to-day operations. You will also find that colleagues become less happy, less efficient and, in some cases, less likely to continue their employment with you.

We are now back to a happier place. Revealing the scores of the Happy Index to the teams is a bit like getting your exam results at school. It's a big deal. The leaders, whether on the shop floor or in the head office, of each team are measured every week on their sales and profit performance but are judged solely on their own, and the wider team's, Happy Index results once a year. If they hit the trading numbers and get a poor Happy Index score there are difficult conversations to be had. The prime focus of the Happy Index is to ensure that all of our colleagues are happy, not solely to drive financial performance. If it was the other way round, I suspect we would have gone bust years ago.

The culture of happiness is not one you can just switch on when the surveys are about to be sent out. It's a complex cultural journey that takes a long time to build, and a brief time to destroy. Essentially, we believe that to be a great leader, and to have a strong culture, you need to know your people, do what you say you're going to do, be kind, and communicate well. This gets you a good Happy Index score.

On a scale of 1–10, how happy are you with the support you get from your manager?

Please tick the appropriate box (1–6 is poor, 7–8 is average, 9–10 is excellent)

	1	2	3	4	5	6	7	8	9	10
Manager										

In order to foster a culture of trust and compassion it is important to measure happiness, and that also means measuring unhappiness. We don't always get it right, and it's a leader's job to know this when it goes wrong. We have lost great colleagues in the past because they have been unfairly treated by their bosses, and this is a scar we have to bear. But with a clear focus on measuring and acting upon surveys such as the Happy Index, you are in a better position than most to be kind, and have colleagues who turn up to work with a spring in their step.

In circulating the Happy Index throughout the entire company, it allows us to get a 30,000-foot view of working processes, and gives us the opportunity to learn how colleagues have responded to our benefits and acts of kindness, but also where we can prevent problems of our own making happening in the future.

We find that if you ask one simple question only, you end up getting a much more honest and informative response. Colleagues often fill pages and pages with their feelings, experiences, and challenges. Many just say 'thank you', while others have a moan. We've learned that the more questions you ask, the less insight you often get into the individual colleagues you're trying to support.

Alongside the Happy Index and other measures that we have in place to amaze our colleagues, we also believe in the importance of operating the business with an outward-looking focus, to see what other companies and industries are doing successfully, what things they are implementing that we admire, and the reasons why those things are or are not working. To stay relevant, you need to constantly evolve and look at your business in the wider context of the planet, society, and local community. The only way to do that is by keeping your eyes and ears open, to colleagues' feedback as well as competitors' schemes, and by getting out to see for yourself how you can bring great ideas to help colleagues back at base camp.

ASK THE PEOPLE ON THE SHOP FLOOR

At the start of each week, I head out to a different part of the country to visit the managers and teams at our branches. Back in 2021, our colleagues were returning from furlough, and we were all set to do what we did best – serve the public. While not all our challenges had disappeared, it always feels better to be relying on ourselves rather than solely depending on external government support for survival, whether that be furlough schemes or apprenticeships.

Visiting the shops has held a special place in my heart since I first took on the role of CEO, and continues to be a source of profound inspiration and invaluable market insights. Typically, I aim to spend three days a week exploring the UK's high streets and retail parks, making visits to over 700 of our shops every year. Conversations with colleagues and helping customers is an integral part of our company routine. However, my curiosity often extends beyond our own stores.

Though vastly different from Richer Sounds, a speciality audio and TV retailer, I often engage in mystery shopping their branches to glean insights from their exemplary customer service. Similarly, a visit to Hotel Chocolat has provided me with an opportunity to admire their high-quality display standards, while independent retailers tend to offer a treasure trove of innovative ideas too. Walking through places like Altrincham

Market, not far from Timpson's headquarters, is always infinitely more inspiring than analysing the balance sheet.

To ensure consistency in terms of customer service and cleanliness, my visits to stores are preferably unannounced. It's better for me to see the shop how a customer sees it. If colleagues know I'm coming, the shop is quickly hoovered, ties are put on, and the work tops dusted down. This isn't real life. Frequently, I walk into one of our shops, pick up a ringing phone, and hear someone say, 'James is in the area.' The element of surprise, however, failed me during a visit to Oban one summer, our most remote shop. I hadn't seen Alistair, our manager, for four years, so I embarked on a three-hour detour to reach the shop, only to discover it was Alistair's day off. Lesson learned: next time, as an exception, I'd give Alistair a call before setting out.

When speaking with colleagues, my questions focus on three fundamental aspects: how did this year's sales compare to the previous year? How could we assist in generating more revenue? And, most crucially, how are they feeling personally? The answer to this last question goes beyond reams of data, doesn't require spreadsheets, and focuses solely on the person, not the shop. Regardless of having the best locations, efficient systems, and data, if our colleagues aren't happy, everything else seems meaningless.

While I lacked any formal qualifications for managing a chain of shops, being the Chairman's son and holding a degree in geography did have its benefits. If I were to specialize in a subject on *Mastermind*, it would, rather unexcitedly, be 'The motorway systems and car parks of Great Britain'. After three decades of shop visits, I've mastered the most efficient travel routes and identified prime parking spots, including an unexpected car park in Harrow with a hole in the fence right behind our shop.

The excitement of visiting shops isn't solely derived from the sound of the cash register opening and the noise of money going into the till; it is equally rooted in reigniting the creative process that makes business so captivating. Even for an old-fashioned shoe repair business like ours, the quest for inspiration is unending.

After experimenting with numerous approaches, I can confidently say that the simplest way to unearth fresh ideas is to consult directly with our colleagues. There is often no need to look further afield. If I were to seek out ways to improve our warehouse efficiency, I wouldn't pore over management accounts while sitting at my desk. Instead, I will simply walk into the warehouse and ask our colleagues – who directly handle the day-to-day operations of the warehouse and our stock – what we need to do.

Historically, retail leaders would often visit their shops on a weekly basis, typically on Fridays, while the remainder of their time was taken up with their responsibilities at the head office, including supplier meetings, data analysis, and looking at the next strategic review. Our approach at Timpson continues to remain distinct: we trust our colleagues on the front line to make decisions. It is not only more cost-effective but also much faster to help in actioning change.

The shopkeepers, those individuals on the floor, are the ones who understand the daily pulse of our operations. If they need help or have suggestions, it is essential that we visit them and discuss those needs directly. This approach is deeply ingrained into our company culture and philosophy, recognizing that the key to the company's day-to-day advancement lies in understanding and supporting the requirements of our colleagues who are on the shop floor. What they say, goes.

Whenever visiting a branch, I try to get stuck in and do some jobs while I'm there. Taking on shoe repairs during these shop visits is not just a nostalgic exercise; it is an opportunity to reconnect with the craft, and understand the needs of our colleagues and customers better. Learning to repair shoes is like learning to ride a bike. It's hard to get going, but when you know it, it never leaves you. However, key cutting is a different skill altogether. Consistent practice is essential to match the correct blank with the appropriate key. Speaking of which, if you were the customer I served in Aylesbury last summer, I think I cut the keys on the wrong blank. I'm sorry!

Serving customers provides the most profound understanding of what is and what isn't working, as well as what is needed to improve our business. After each visit, I compile extensive lists and photos of issues to address, and innovative ideas presented by our colleagues to explore. It is a stark reminder, and one that business leaders must be aware of, that the real heart of any business is on the front line, not within the confines of an office. The front line is your marketing, PR, buying, and training department in one.

The more we travel, meet up for a coffee or a meal, share stories, ideas, and experiences, the greater our chances of discovering new avenues for improving our businesses. Those who serve our customers are the true architects of our success, and their experiences and insights are invaluable in shaping our futures.

EMBRACE SOCIETAL CHANGES TO REMAIN RELEVANT

When my great-great-grandfather, William Timpson, opened his first shop in Manchester in 1865, it's safe to say he had different concerns than those we grapple with today. If he were to glance at the minutes of our most recent board meeting, I doubt he'd find any resonance with the topics under discussion. Questions like *'Do we have enough mental health first aiders?'* and *'How can we reduce our carbon footprint?'* would be utterly at odds with his nineteenth-century operations – concepts and ideas important to today that would never have crossed the mind of any business person in his era.

Running a business today is a far more intricate affair than it was in 1865. A Chief Executive's inbox isn't just overflowing with financial reports; it's inundated with updates on diversity initiatives, online reviews, and health and safety compliance. With these expanded responsibilities comes the need for leaders to acquire additional skills, ensuring that the company both adheres to regulations and serves as a responsible corporate citizen.

Over the past decade, many taboos have been shattered, none more important than those surrounding mental health in the workplace. We all now recognize the significance of supporting colleagues dealing with mental health challenges in and out of the workplace, which is why it is brilliant to see so many companies now including company-driven schemes and additional services that put people's livelihoods first as part of the job offer package.

The benefits are clear: when colleagues receive the support they need and recover, they tend to stay with us for the long haul.

However, there remains another taboo – a topic that requires more attention: the menopause.

The menopause affects 51 per cent of our population, but its impact reverberates throughout every corner of society. It's a subject that had seldom been broached, until recently. While far too little is known about it, there has been a greater public interest in the topic thanks to the likes of Davina McCall and Louise Newsom who have been empowering people going through the menopause to discuss it more openly, whether that be personally or professionally. If companies were to take a proactive approach, opening the door to what may initially be uncomfortable conversations, we could be far more effective in supporting the fastest-growing demographic in our workforce.

The menopause is the result of a natural and prolonged decline in the hormone oestrogen, resulting in a long-term hormonal deficiency that can result in a host of unpleasant symptoms. However, these troublesome symptoms of menopause are frequently underrecognized, undervalued, and not taken seriously.

Symptoms like hot flushes, fatigue, mood swings, and cognitive fog don't just affect home life and personal relationships; they impact careers as well. The average age at which a woman typically begins experiencing noticeable symptoms of the menopause is 51, and it can persist for approximately seven years, though some endure it for decades. Shockingly, 78 per cent of women don't even recognize their symptoms as menopause-related, making it unsurprising that many managers fail to provide the appropriate support. Ill-informed managers often misinterpret these symptoms as work-related performance issues, not health-related challenges, and this misunderstanding exacerbates the problem. It's also disconcerting to observe the gender pay gap widening as women enter the menopausal stage.

The way menopause affects women's health varies as much as companies' responses to supporting them. When nearly half of your menopausal workforce considers early retirement and 9 per cent face disciplinary actions due to their symptoms, it's evident that we have much to learn. The performance issue isn't because women have suddenly become less competent at their jobs; it's because they are experiencing menopause.

Successful employment tribunals against employers who failed to support female colleagues during menopause are already on the rise. This trend will only become more common unless companies become better informed and take proactive steps to provide support.

The initial step that companies should take is to foster a culture where women can openly discuss their concerns, and managers feel comfortable and well-informed enough to listen. By extending a hand of understanding, many women will feel reassured that their symptoms won't lead to disciplinary action and job termination but will instead lead to the support they need to excel in their roles.

Simple, low-cost measures, such as providing desk fans, allowing time off for medical appointments, or offering the opportunity to speak with a colleague trained in menopause support, can make a significant difference. Implementing a comprehensive menopause policy alongside a designated menopause champion, preferably a female colleague who has experienced menopause, can help embed support into the company's culture.

Effective treatment can dramatically enhance someone's quality of life. The most well-known treatment is hormone replacement therapy (HRT), yet only 10 per cent of women opt for it, despite clear evidence that the benefits, such as reduced time off and increased productivity, outweigh any risks.

While it's not a company's responsibility to dispense HRT drugs, it is our duty to help colleagues access advice, and create a culture where they feel comfortable seeking help. Partnering with menopause experts enables us to guide colleagues toward the crucial steps to finding tailored support. Organizations like The Menopause Charity and the Balance app are excellent sources of information to assist women and their employers.

There are shining examples of companies leading the way in addressing menopause-related challenges. Companies like Next, HSBC, and Bruntwood have embraced proactive approaches and, in return, have seen reduced staff turnover and increased productivity. It's astounding that many companies have yet to dive into this essential discussion.

Citation, a Cheshire-based HR support company serving small and medium-sized enterprises (SMEs) across the UK, is at the forefront of this movement. More and more clients are heeding their advice and reaping the benefits. The once-closed door is slowly swinging open.

My hope is that more companies will become well-informed about menopause, and understand what they can do to better support colleagues who are grappling with it. We've made significant strides in caring for our colleagues, and it's time to take the next step, embracing the challenges and opportunities that menopause presents. A good way to start is appointing someone as your menopause champion.

Other ways to make positive change

What's clear is that to lead a great company, your arms need to be open to change. Employers need to celebrate people's differences and be aware of the challenges they and the world faces. Recently we have been supporting a colleague as they transition, and have committed to recruiting more Afghan refugees. These aren't just actions to be ultra inclusive, they are actions because we want to find and support great people. Change also comes from changing laws and customer expectations. Our drive to reduce our carbon usage has led to all our new company cars being electric, and plastic bags have been completely phased out. What was once unusual and unknown, quickly becomes the norm.

Serving customers provides the most profound understanding of what is and what isn't working.

UPSIDE-DOWN MANAGEMENT IN ACTION

Up until the 1960s, the majority of Glasgow shut down for the last two weeks of July for what was known as the Glasgow Fair, which was largely due to colleagues heading off on holidays, meaning no one was there to man the shops. As I was getting to grips with the business, my grandfather was prone to telling me to avoid visiting our Glasgow branches during this holiday period – it was better going to Blackpool where the Glaswegians were spending their money.

It wasn't until 1938 that UK law changed, allowing workers a one-week paid holiday, prior to this date any holidays taken by employees were unpaid. However, bosses quickly began to recognize the important role that holidays play in the wellbeing of their colleagues. After giving their people more time off, bosses soon discovered that the people working for them were happier and more productive thanks to this law change. Of course, and quite rightly, things have moved on a fair bit since the mid-twentieth century and now, across the board, everyone who is working is given a minimum of 28 days paid holiday, which is an essential ingredient for a good quality of life.

A friend of mine, who runs a tech company in San Francisco, told me that to recruit the best coders their standard employment offer now includes – aside from the eye-watering salaries – complementary Ubers to and from work, free food cooked by a top chef, and *unlimited* holidays. You read that right: unlimited holidays. Their top coder has also agreed that he can go home when it's raining.

This got me wondering how many days those coders would take when their holiday is unlimited, compared to the disheartening statistic provided by Personnel Today about annual leave here in the UK, where team members tend to take just 62 per cent of their holiday entitlement throughout the year. That means some people are losing out on close to an additional two weeks of annual leave, which would allow them to take a break from work, relax with their families, and return to work feeling refreshed and ready to work.

It is hugely important that individuals take their allocated holidays for their physical and mental wellbeing. I doubt anyone on their death bed believes that they should have spent more time in the office . . .

John Spedan Lewis, son of the department store founder, was one of the first to recognize the importance of holidays, and how to help employees have a break at the company's expense. It may be because his father refused to take any holidays at all that John, in 1937, opened the first colleague holiday camp in the grounds of his Leckford Estate in Hampshire. He wanted to share the beautiful location with those who worked so hard for him and his family to be able to afford it in the first place. Today the partnership, despite recent financial problems, has five fantastic holiday locations across the UK, as well as a yacht for partners and their families.

Over the last 15 years, inspired by both John Lewis and Richer Sounds, we now have a fleet of 19 holiday homes across the UK that are available all year round for any colleagues looking to book breaks with their families. To me this is what enlightened capitalism is about, and while expensive, it can be the best money a business can spend.

The average family spends two months' salary on their holi-days, so if my colleagues can spend time in a relaxing place, knowing that the company is picking up the tab, it's only going to help in enticing fantastic prospective candidates, and retaining the very best of people.

Initially, we made an inauspicious start and, without doing any research, I purchased a 21-bedroom seaside hotel in Anglesey. Everyone in the company loved the idea of a free holiday, but they sadly didn't want to spend it with their colleagues. They enjoyed working together, but the idea of going on holiday together was a step too far. Instead, they wanted a quiet lodge on a family friendly holiday park.

Unsure of what to do with the site in Anglesey, and the 70 acres that came with it, we knocked it down and replaced it with a restaurant. We had no wish to get into the hotel busi-ness at the time but the unintended result of my naive purchase was the creation of a successful venture, The Oyster Catcher, that now employs 80 local people. It was a lucky escape.

The inspiration for this was Jamie Oliver, the well-known chef and entrepreneur. He set up the Fifteen Foundation in 2004 to help train disadvantaged people in the hospitality industry. Jamie and his team developed a small number of restaurants with the sole purpose of both offering great hospi-tality, while training young people in cheffing and front of house skills. It inspired a TV show and diners flocked to support the initiative. It sat well with my views on second chances, so we copied the idea when The Oyster Catcher opened its doors.

Having taken on board everyone's feedback regarding where they'd like to go on holiday, we instead invested in lodges that were close to National Parks and coastal areas, which cost between £90,000–130,000. They all come with great facilities, such as indoor pools and mini golf, and for any colleagues who want to spend their holidays here, we ask only that they pay for their travel and any food and drink they'll need, while the rest – including a chilled bottle of fizz in the fridge – is all on us.

It hasn't always been plain sailing, but we've now got a system in place to manage bookings at the lodges, which is open to every single colleague throughout the business, catering for their specific requirements. Despite not wanting to revitalize the hotel in Anglesey, the lodges are a bit like running a hotel! There are three lodges where dogs are allowed to accompany their owners, and we have six that are wheelchair friendly. All the properties are regularly cleaned and, at the end of each stay, we ask every colleague what we could do to improve the experience for next time. Company culture is important at work, of course, but when you are also providing services outside of the workplace as well, it's important to provide families with their best holiday of the year.

Financially, the total cash cost to the company after buying the sites, made up mostly of benefit in kind (a tax on looking after your colleagues), is around £500,000 a year. So that's under £20k per holiday home and after the weekly shop bonus it's considered the best benefit the company offers. It's impossible to prove that every penny we spend on holiday homes is wise, but the postcards and thank you letters (often written by children), and seeing the smiling faces of colleagues who've just returned from a week's break are enough to know it's money well spent.

Spedan Lewis was right. Those who help you to make money should get the holidays they deserve.

What Have We Learned?

Learning from successful companies
To stay ahead in the business world, it's crucial to study successful companies. Timpson looks to industry leaders like Greggs, John Lewis and Richer Sounds for inspiration, adapting their customer-centric approaches to continually improve their own services.

Adaptability
Successful businesses are those that can pivot and embrace change while staying true to their core values. Timpson's ability to adapt during the Covid pandemic exemplifies this principle.

The Happy Index
Using this simple one-question survey to measure happiness ensures colleagues' wellbeing is a top priority. Managers, leaders, and colleagues are judged based on the Happy Index results, not on their financial performance.

Understanding daily operations
The people on the shop floor, those who understand daily operations, are instrumental in driving the company's success. Decisions made in the boardroom often have little impact or benefit.

Embrace societal changes
Keep on top of any changes within the wider society, such as mental health, the impact of menopause, and the rising cost of

living in order to support colleagues and remain a relevant and attractive company to potential employees.

Avoiding the wrong side of panic

Avoid being in prolonged periods of panic in business operations that could cause morale to fall and financial successes to dip. Being just on the right side of panic is the most profitable and fun place to be.

Listening to feedback

Timpson listens to colleagues' feedback and adjusts its offerings based on what they tell us, exemplifying the importance of valuing individual needs. If it's important to a colleague, it's important to you too.

Enlightened capitalism

Timpson's approach to providing free holidays for colleagues aligns with the concept of enlightened capitalism, where companies invest in employee wellbeing and satisfaction.

Financial investment for colleague happiness

Despite the financial cost, Timpson views benefits that make colleagues' lives that little bit easier as a valuable investment that results in companywide happiness and wellbeing

THE STATE AND THE STREET: A STORY OF GOVERNMENT AND BUSINESS

Welcome to **Lesson Four**, where we dive deep into the challenges and transformations of the high street in the modern era. In this lesson, we will examine the evolving landscape of high streets across the UK, exploring the impact of factors such as Covid, changing consumer habits, and economic disparities between regions.

The high street, once a vibrant hub the community, has faced existential challenges in recent years. **Lesson Four** is your guide to understanding the intricacies of these challenges and potential solutions that can breathe new life into our beloved high streets. Like all sectors, the landscape in which we operate is continually changing, and it's a leader's job to try to keep up and survive. If you don't work in retail, I'm sure you can relate to how structural changes in your own industry have had an impact on you, and how you need to adapt and evolve.

We'll begin by analysing the effects of the Covid pandemic on the high street, highlighting the role of government interventions, such as the suspension on evictions, and sustaining businesses during difficult times. We will also discuss the evolving relationship between landlords and tenants, examining how new leasing practices are reshaping the high street's dynamics.

Lesson Four doesn't stop at diagnosing the issues. We'll explore real-world examples of towns and cities that have successfully revitalized their high streets; demonstrating that with vision and community engagement, positive change is possible. These studies will provide valuable insights into the potential strategies that can help high streets thrive once again.

Additionally, we will address the impending challenges posed by business rates, a looming tsunami that threatens high streets across the nation. We'll discuss the need for bold decisions and visionary policymaking to ensure the survival and prosperity of high streets in the face of this economic storm.

The role of suppliers and partners in supporting a business through the highs and lows is often overlooked. We will look at how a strategy of being both kind and commercial will help you weather the storms, and help you stay on the right side of panic.

Lesson Four invites you to join us on a journey through the high street's past, present, and future. By the end of this lesson, you will have a comprehensive understanding of the complex web of factors affecting high streets, as well as actionable insights into how to navigate these challenges, and contribute to the resurgence of these vital community centres. In some ways, it's a lesson in how you survive when everything around you keeps changing.

BUILDING STRONG RELATIONSHIPS WITH SUPPLIERS

Respecting and valuing our suppliers, consumers, and colleagues is not only the ethical way to conduct business but also the most profitable approach. The success of any enterprise hinges on three crucial factors: having exceptional colleagues, satisfied customers, and reliable suppliers. Striking a harmonious balance among these elements can be challenging, but it's essential to avoid exploiting suppliers due to the perceived vulnerability in the relationship.

Much like we gauge a society by how it treats its poorest citizens, we can evaluate a company by its treatment of suppliers. A friend once shared a valuable insight with me – being a good buyer entails dealing with people you trust and admire, and when the margins are favourable, refraining from excessive negotiations. Ultimately, it's not solely about what the supplier produces; what truly matters is the value generated. If you're happy with what you're making from a product you buy, stop negotiating.

However, it's worth noting that some suppliers fall short, by making exaggerated promises or overextending themselves. I recall one supplier who flaunted their newfound wealth in a brand-new Ferrari outside our office, boasting about his earnings from our account to the receptionist. Such naivety inevitably led to the termination of our business relationship.

Challenges faced by suppliers

While it's crucial for companies to treat their suppliers well, it's equally important to understand the challenges suppliers face in the modern business landscape. Many suppliers are now burdened with compliance requirements, including detailed audits and bureaucratic processes that often add little value. This excessive red tape can sap the joy out of doing business.

Consider the case of a supplier charged £1,500 a day for inspections by an outsourced auditor. After two days, they received an A grade. However, the same auditor returned the next day, now working for a different customer, asking the same questions and awarding another A grade. This example highlights the duplicative and costly nature of compliance demands.

While large retailers may demand suppliers answer over 500 questions to even get an appointment, some discount retailers demonstrate a more efficient approach. They partner with ethical suppliers and focus on essentials, simplifying operations and reducing costs. Consider this example: if I purchase a truckload of cushions, requesting minimal paperwork and prompt payment within 10 working days, I'll likely secure a competitive price. By facilitating smooth transactions, I enable the supplier to keep their costs down too. Conversely, a competitor's stringent demands, including multiple delivery locations, fines for paperwork discrepancies, mandatory independent audits, and delayed payments inevitably inflate the supplier's costs, which are then passed on to customers.

Fostering trust and collaboration with suppliers

At Timpson, we understand the value of strong supplier relationships. We spend over £2 million a week with our suppliers, and while we may not be perfect, we strive to be the best company they do business with. To set the tone for our business dealings, we have a suppliers' manual that outlines our operating procedures and required documentation. My mobile number is included at the bottom of the remittance advice for immediate problem resolution. Monthly, I meet with our finance team to ensure prompt payment to our suppliers, as timely compensation is integral to our pact with each supplier. We reject the practice of using suppliers as an alternative source of financing, recognizing that it is unfair and unethical. The quicker we pay our suppliers, the more accurate and speedier their deliveries seem to be.

Our commitment to fostering trust and collaboration was put to the test during the uncertainty of the Covid pandemic. When our shops were forced to close, we had no idea what the future held for our business. In a show of solidarity, I personally called all our main suppliers and assured them that they would be paid in full, even though we couldn't predict when we could place another order. This trust and goodwill we had built over the years helped us support each other, and I am pleased to say that none of our suppliers went out of business. This experience demonstrated that both companies and suppliers can thrive when they act ethically and support one another.

The same happened with our landlords. We wrote to all of them to say we had signed a lease agreement in good faith, and although difficult we would pay our rents in full, unless they felt they wanted to share the pain of Covid with us. Most landlords gave little or no discount, but they remembered that we were 'good for the money'. Looking at the level of rents we now pay post Covid, we are seeing huge reductions because we are one of the few tenants who they know will always pay their bills. Even though it was never the plan, paying our rent when it was difficult has saved us millions when times are much easier.

Reciprocity in business relationships

The principle of reciprocity plays a crucial role in business relationships. Just as we appreciated landlords who provided rent reductions during the challenging times of the pandemic, it's essential to recognize and reciprocate acts of kindness and support. We wrote thank-you letters to these landlords, expressing our gratitude for their generosity. Their responses were heartwarming and highlighted the significance of acknowledging and appreciating the contributions of others in our business ecosystem.

This practice of reciprocity can have a profound impact on future negotiations and collaborations. When it comes to the next rent negotiation, we know that our history of gratitude and appreciation will lead to more generous and mutually beneficial agreements.

Celebrating strong supplier relationships

The pinnacle of our supplier engagement efforts is our annual suppliers' lunch, where we invite over 200 guests to celebrate our relationship. Unlike some companies that convene suppliers solely to negotiate further discounts, our approach is to express our gratitude and appreciation. In the world of shoe repair, this event is akin to the Oscars.

During the event, we provide updates on our business performance, outline our plans for the year ahead, and present awards that recognize the invaluable contributions our suppliers have made to our success. Without them, we simply wouldn't have a business to celebrate. This event serves as a tangible expression of our commitment to treating our suppliers as true partners. If we take Wilko, for example, who have not been able to pay their suppliers after their recent liquidation, it creates a sense of mistrust between them and the people they serve.

Treating suppliers, consumers, and colleagues with respect is not only the right thing to do but also a strategic imperative for long-term success and profitability. Companies that prioritize respect and ethical business practices create an environment where trust and collaboration thrive, leading to mutually beneficial outcomes for all stakeholders.

By valuing and supporting our suppliers, we can streamline operations, reduce costs, and ultimately deliver better products and services to our customers. This approach not only strengthens business relationships but also fosters a culture of integrity and sustainability.

In an ever-evolving business landscape, the power of respect should not be underestimated. It has the potential to transform companies, build enduring partnerships, and contribute to a more ethical and prosperous business environment.

Your life should not be determined by where you live.

NEW ECONOMIC CHALLENGES

In every industry, there are key numbers and formulas that define success. These metrics provide a framework for businesses to operate efficiently and sustainably. For instance, in the hospitality industry, wages should ideally constitute around 30 per cent of sales, with the cost of food and drink not exceeding 30 per cent either. When you add in 10 per cent for variable costs, and another 10 per cent for rent, it leaves you with a 10 per cent profit margin. In our retail business, these figures are roughly the same. However, what used to be a relatively straightforward endeavour in aligning these figures has recently become more akin to navigating a turbulent sea, with the advent of factors like Covid and Brexit. As we move forward, we must adapt and rethink our operating models in order to stay afloat in this new reality.

Before delving deeper into these challenges, it's worth taking a step back to appreciate the historical context. In August 1975, inflation in the UK soared to just under 27 per cent. To control costs, the Government imposed a salary increase cap of £6 per week for workers. This cap, while well-intentioned, had an unintended consequence on businesses, particularly retailers. Shop assistants, who were earning a mere £10 per week, saw a 60 per cent immediate increase in their wages. The resulting rise in operating costs had a significant impact on shopkeepers, forcing them to cut costs wherever possible and raise prices multiple times a year. It was a survival tactic during a period of extreme economic volatility. In essence, not raising prices was not an option – it was a path to insolvency.

Fast forward to today, and we're grappling with a different set of economic challenges, shaped by global factors beyond our control. One of the most pressing concerns is the state of the shipping market, which has been upended. In 2020, the cost of shipping a container, for instance, skyrocketed from $2,000 to a staggering $17,000. Fortunately, we're now back to the much more attractive price of less than $1,500. This increase was driven by a complex interplay of factors, including disruptions in the supply chain, labour shortages, and larger container ships that take longer to unload. At times it felt like shipping companies were making up the prices on a daily basis, and then doubling them.

In the UK, it used to take only a few days to unload a ship at a port. Now, due to the increasing size of ships and labour shortages at docks, it can take up to two weeks. This not only delays deliveries but also raises costs significantly. Similar disruptions are echoed further up the supply chain. Chinese suppliers, with whom we've had long-standing relationships, are under immense pressure to increase their prices. Despite our best efforts in negotiations, we are facing price hikes of at least 5 per cent and sometimes even more. The primary driver behind these increases is the booming Chinese domestic market, which has caused internal demand for products to outstrip supply.

Interestingly, the rising wages in China parallel a similar trend in the UK. In London, delivery drivers now earn more than EasyJet pilots, chefs are enjoying 20 per cent pay hikes just to retain them, and specialist web developers are frequently offered 50 per cent pay increases to switch to competitors. The labour market, especially in the South-East, is highly competitive, making recruitment challenging. In our own company, we typically have only a handful of vacancies, but that number can at times surge. In this situation, it's tempting to hire quickly and compromise on the qualities we seek in our colleagues. However, we are committed to hiring only superstars; individuals who we consistently rate 9 or 10 out of 10. We'd rather leave a vacancy open than hire someone who doesn't meet our high standards. Our colleagues deserve to work alongside individuals who are just as remarkable as they are.

To address these challenges, we have devised a two-pronged plan. First, we understand that price increases are inevitable, but we intend to delay them for as long as possible. Instead, we have chosen to increase the wages of our colleagues. We recently announced a 5 per cent pay raise and then an extra £2,000 for every employee in the company. We hope this means our colleagues can keep up with the costs of living and see us as an attractive place to work. While this may not have a major impact on the Bank of England's calculation of future inflation, it will help us attract and retain our talented workforce.

With the National Living Wage rising to £11.44 in April 2024, similar wage increases are likely to become commonplace across the country. We normally give every colleague a pay review on the anniversary of when they joined the company, but we may need to look at doing this twice a year, if inflation remains high. This is a positive development, as paying employees as generously as possible is not just a business decision; it's the right thing to do.

In line with this philosophy, we believe that companies that prioritize fair compensation, employee wellbeing, and a culture of kindness will not only weather the storms we currently face but also emerge stronger. But you need to be brave. The message is clear: during challenging times, companies that invest in their people, internally or externally, and who foster a culture of care and support are the ones that will thrive.

Now, let's turn our attention to the broader retail industry and the high street. These are sectors facing their own unique set of challenges, compounded by the recent disruptions in the global economy. In the midst of these changes, it's crucial to understand the evolving dynamics of the retail landscape and how businesses, like Timpson, are adapting.

DEAR CHANCELLOR, FIX THE COST OF RATES FOR US RETAILERS

In today's retail landscape, the most influential player on the high street isn't the tenants or the landlords; it's the Chancellor. The moratorium on a landlord's ability to boot a tenant out, introduced by Rishi Sunak in Covid, played a pivotal role in preventing mass evictions, and sustaining the operations of many retailers, including myself. However, when the Government steps into an established complex market and dictates how it should work, it takes time for everything to readjust. A market works best when there is an equal balance between suppliers and customers. When the Government joins the party, problems start, and these are hard to remove.

The traditional landlord-tenant dynamic, akin to a feudal system, has been the backbone of the retail property market for decades. While it may not be perfect, it has adapted to the ever-changing dynamics of supply and demand, resulting in fair valuations for the retail spaces we operate from. Shopkeepers have perennially grumbled about their rent, but market forces have typically determined the prevailing rates. However, times are changing, and rents are no longer on an upward trajectory.

When I embarked on my retail journey in 1995, signing 25-year leases for shops was commonplace – a significant commitment that landlords and their financial backers cherished. After all, who wouldn't appreciate a guaranteed income spanning a quarter of a century? But times have evolved, and today we are more inclined to sign 5-year leases with a break clause at year 3. Landlords have recognized the shifting market dynamics and are content as long as the rent, though lower, continues to flow in.

One silver lining of the Covid moratorium was that it brought landlords and tenants closer together. We, as retailers, engaged in conversations with landlords whom we previously only received bills from. By bypassing agents and communicating directly with tenants, landlords gained a better understanding of the challenges we face. They've realized that being more intimately connected to their tenants (or customers, as I prefer to call them) is mutually beneficial. I find it's always better dealing with a landlord face-to-face when there is an issue, rather than through expensive letters a lawyer has written.

Across the UK, landlords have demonstrated remarkable adaptability during the Covid pandemic. Approximately 45 per cent of all retail leases were fully honoured, 45 per cent were renegotiated, and for the remaining 10 per cent, it boiled down to a question of inability or unwillingness to pay. Some retailers chose not to pay when they could, while others were probably going to close their doors whether there had been Covid or not. Either way, the moratorium led to over £6 billion in unpaid rent.

It's important to acknowledge that while the moratorium was crucial for certain sectors, it only constitutes a small slice of the overall pie. If I were a landlord with a property previously occupied by a nightclub, banned from reopening due to Covid restrictions, I wouldn't expect the full rent. However, I would anticipate an open and honest conversation, to maximize rent while providing a lifeline to the operator. Government grants and rate holidays injected money into the system. As a landlord, I stand to gain when doors reopen, and tills ring again. But if my tenant goes bankrupt, I would need to offer even more incentives to attract a new, unknown operator. It's economically wiser to stick with a tenant I know.

At Timpson, our approach was simple and principled. We have honoured the agreements we've signed while seeking assistance that was available. We requested monthly payments instead of quarterly, and 99 per cent of landlords agreed. Furthermore, we expected the same terms that were granted to other tenants if landlords were supporting them. More than half of our shops now have new agreements in place, aiding our financial stability during what were unforeseen challenges. Our landlords can see that we possess a strong covenant and, as they say in the trade, 'are good for the rent'.

This approach aligns with our core strategy – to build long-term relationships through understanding and kindness with everyone we engage with. Many landlords are not large institutions but families who rely on the rental income for retirement and supporting their children.

Regrettably, some retailers have viewed the moratorium as an opportunity to exert undue pressure on their landlords, withholding rent and, in some cases, forcing landlords into liquidation. Some of the biggest names on the high street are guilty of this approach. While it may have been a calculated business decision for them, it ultimately comes down to moral principles. With government support through furlough schemes, business rate holidays, and state backed loans, most businesses could afford to pay at least some of the rent. Those who did not play their part, especially when reporting significant profits and bonuses afterward, failed in their moral responsibility.

To illustrate the impact of these changes, the average new rents at lease renewal, negotiated by my fantastic team in our Estates office in Lutterworth, have dropped by over 30 per cent, and the trend is continuing. This reduction has occurred without factoring in the frequent addition of six months of rent-free periods, and other incentives thrown our way. I believe that the market has adapted well, and that a number of well-known property owners are reluctant to give deals to those retailers that played the 'tough guy' card in Covid. The phrase 'penny wise, pound foolish' comes to mind when thinking of some of these retailers who are now faced with much higher rents than they should be paying, purely as a result of their poor behaviour.

Experience has taught us that the property market is not for the faint-hearted. Signing a lease, using your home as collateral, and paying rent month after month is a daunting prospect, and for some, it's a risk not worth taking. As a nation of shopkeepers, we understand this gamble, but when the market experiences turmoil as it did so unexpectedly, there is a need for a spirit of generosity and compromise. In most disputes, compromise is the path to resolution, and it is not a sign of weakness to give a little in order to gain a lot.

It's a system that everyone agrees is broken, but we haven't had a visionary politician who is prepared to take on the challenge yet. Now is the time to address what has long been the 'high income can' kicked down the road by countless Chancellors. Bold decisions were made to save our high streets during the Covid pandemic, and now, similarly brave decisions are needed to ensure their survival in the future.

Wilko's Decline – Lessons for High Street Survival

The decline of Wilko, a fellow retailer and family business, serves as a sombre reminder of the challenges facing the high street. With over 12,000 jobs at risk, empty storefronts in town centres, and the ripple effect on suppliers and landlords, Wilko's downfall raised questions about the future of our traditional shopping districts.

Wilko's demise can be attributed to a combination of misguided strategy and ineffective leadership. However, it's crucial to view this as an isolated case rather than a sign of impending doom for all high streets. Instead, it underscores the dynamism of the retail market and how competitors can outpace those who fail to adapt.

In 2013, Wilko unveiled a new concept store in Fulham Broadway station with great fanfare. At the same time, their competitors like B&M, Home Bargains, and Poundland were focusing on large out-of-town stores while overlooking online retailing. I remember walking past this shop and saying to myself 'What have they done?' Wilko misread the shift in consumer behaviour and tried to be too upmarket in their ranges. This divergence in strategy would prove to be a critical misstep.

Furthermore, a revolving door of management changes failed to halt Wilko's declining sales. While they invested in expensive distribution centres, the ongoing cost-of-living crisis instead required a focus on offering low prices and basic retailing, both of which they struggled to deliver effectively.

The collapse of a major retail business inevitably grabs headlines, but beneath the surface, our high streets and out-of-town shopping centres are constantly evolving, with positive changes often going unnoticed. As someone who spends a substantial amount of time visiting shops, I see the retail landscape evolving rapidly. Rather than witnessing a crisis, I observe a market in transformation, and my confidence in its ability to shape a bright future has never been stronger. Despite the turbulence from Covid, the retail landscape is back on the front foot.

Let's examine one crucial aspect of this transformation: rents. At Timpson, we benefit from an exceptional in-house team of surveyors who consistently negotiate with landlords to secure the best possible deals. While their primary task was once to limit rent increases, the tables have turned, and the goal now is to secure substantial rent reductions. Over the past six months, high street rents have again dropped on average by 32 per cent – a clear indicator that market forces are at work. Even in prosperous towns like Cambridge and Farnham, we've witnessed declining rents. This shift presents challenges for landlords, who are increasingly willing to accept lower rents in exchange for occupied spaces. As a result, independent retailers are more likely to take a chance on these spaces, enhancing the diversity and vibrancy of our shopping areas.

While online sales are crucial in the modern retail landscape, there's a growing emphasis on encouraging customers to visit physical stores for order collection. In our Max Spielmann photo business, more than 80 per cent of online orders are now collected in-store. This not only saves on postage costs but also provides an opportunity to sell related products like frames or albums.

The key to success in the retail industry lies in having a motivated and content workforce that delivers exceptional service. Great colleagues who are committed to providing outstanding customer experiences set remarkable retailers apart. Perhaps a stronger focus on this aspect could have made a difference for Wilko as it grappled with the changing retail landscape.

Addressing regional disparities

One of the most glaring disparities in the UK is the difference in financial investments between the North and the South. Affluent areas often receive more attention and resources, leaving economically deprived areas struggling to keep up. This divide is not only an economic issue but also a social one. Timpson, as a company committed to hiring ex-offenders and giving back to the community, understands that your life should not be determined by where you live.

We have shops in every different type of demographic area in the UK. In fact, we are fortunate that the products we sell are popular across the whole of the country. In some ways, we are a bit like Gregg's. What I see is that the poorer towns and cities I go to on shop visits generally get less investment from Westminster. I can see why private developers want to focus on wealthier areas as they will make more money, but the Government has a responsibility to treat all citizens as equals, no matter where they live.

In affluent areas, the high street may appear vibrant and thriving, with a diverse range of shops and services catering to the needs and desires of the well-off residents. However, in lower socio-economic areas, the high street may tell a different story – one of boarded-up shops and a lack of opportunities. It's not our job to solve this problem, but we need to keep supporting our colleagues no matter where they live and no matter what chances they have had in life.

THE FUTURE OF THE HIGH STREET

Timpson's approach to revitalizing the high street involves a commitment to adaptability and community engagement. While the company has primarily expanded its portfolio outside of town centres in recent years, the trend could reverse, particularly if developers focus on creating fresh food markets, service arcades, and craft centres. Town centres that take calculated risks and reinvent themselves will witness a resurgence of foot traffic. Online shopping may remain popular, but the lessons learned during the pandemic underscore the importance of personal contact. Every town needs a social hub – a place where people can connect, shop, dine, and interact. The high street, in this context, is not dead; it's evolving faster than ever before.

The challenges facing the high street and the broader retail industry are multifaceted. They are shaped by economic disparities, changing consumer habits, and global disruptions. However, these challenges also present opportunities for innovation, adaptation, and community-driven initiatives. By repurposing high street spaces, embracing lower rents, and fostering community engagement, high streets can not only survive but thrive in the years to come.

As we navigate these turbulent waters, it's clear that the high street's survival depends on the collective efforts of businesses, local councils, and visionary leaders. The high street isn't just a place to shop; it's a reflection of our communities, and a testament to our resilience in the face of change. To ensure its future, we must continue to adapt, innovate, and invest in the wellbeing of our people and our towns. Only then can we look forward to a high street that remains at the heart of our communities, serving as a vibrant and thriving hub for all.

Repurposing high street spaces

To breathe new life into high streets, we need to shift our perspective. The high street should not be viewed merely as a row of shops but as a collection of versatile buildings that can be repurposed to meet the evolving needs of a community. These buildings can become homes, gyms, libraries, or any other space that serves a purpose for today's needs. The key is adaptability. Timpson recognizes the potential for repurposing and adapting high street spaces to align with the changing demands of consumers. This flexibility is essential for the survival and rejuvenation of high streets.

In addition to lower rents, some local councils are taking proactive steps to reduce the number of shops, and create spaces that better align with how people live today. Government support through initiatives like the Towns Fund and the Future High Streets Fund signals a commitment to revitalizing high streets. However, the success of these efforts ultimately hinges on visionary leaders with a deep under-standing of their local communities.

Case Studies in Transformation

To illustrate the potential of high street transformation, let's look at a few inspiring case studies:

Crossgar, Northern Ireland

For a decade, the high street in Crossgar was marred by boarded-up shops, signalling a town in decline. However, a 20-unit social housing development replaced these vacant shops, completely revitalizing the area. The transformation breathed new life into the town and instilled a sense of pride in the community. Crossgar demonstrated that sometimes, a high street doesn't need as many shops as it once had.

Maidenhead, Berkshire

The Nicholsons Shopping Centre in Maidenhead is undergoing a comprehensive regeneration project. This initiative seeks to transform an obsolete, 1960s single-use centre into a vibrant, mixed-use town centre. Hundreds of new homes and workspaces will replace the outdated shopping centre, marking one of the first 'shopping centre to town centre' transformations in the UK.

Altrincham, Greater Manchester

Altrincham faced the daunting task of competing with both a bustling city centre and a massive shopping mall nearby at The

Trafford Centre. However, the modernization of Altrincham's market played a pivotal role in the town's rejuvenation. Owner-managed shops, unique independent food stores, and bustling restaurants and bars have transformed Altrincham into a vibrant market town. The streets are once again bustling with activity, making it a destination worth visiting.

Pavilion Road, London

Pavilion Road, a small mews off Sloane Square developed by Cadogan Estates, showcases a unique shopping experience. Every shop and café is operated by independent businesses, benefiting from relatively low rents. Cadogan Estates recognizes the positive impact of this bustling mews on nearby properties it owns on the King's Road and on Sloane Street, where rents are considerably higher. When I last visited Pavilion Road it was so busy, I could hardly walk through.

THE LONG-FORGOTTEN ENVY OF THE UK'S PENSION SCHEME

Not very long ago, UK company pensions were the envy of Europe, if not the world. My great-grandfather was justly proud of the scheme he established to reward colleagues for their loyalty and help them through retirement. But Robert Maxwell's raid on the Mirror Group Pension Scheme, in a desperate attempt to prop up his ailing business, singlehandedly changed the pension world forever. Maxwell passed away in 1991, and in 2004, the Pensions Regulator officially opened its doors for business. What Maxwell started, the Regulator is now overseeing.

At our recent Trustees' meeting, our advisers from First Actuarial, who we hold in high regard, mentioned the word 'regulator' a staggering 63 times. It has become increasingly evident that the Trustees' primary role is to manage the scheme on behalf of the Regulator rather than for the 1,100 members who rely on it for their retirement security. Healthy company pension schemes like ours, are grappling with the weight of progressively burdensome regulations, and it appears that, over time, many of these schemes will cease to exist.

To illustrate how absurd the situation has become, let me provide a few examples. In 2008, following the global financial crisis, the Regulator urged schemes like ours to reduce risk and allocate a substantial portion of their investments into gilts, which is government backed debt. Had we followed this advice, we would now be facing the same underfunding challenges that most pension schemes now confront, locking in significant losses and plunging our fund into permanent deficit. For context, our scheme has £130 million in assets and a surplus of £43 million.

Ironically, this healthy surplus has become somewhat of a dilemma. While the evidence overwhelmingly supports the long-term outperformance of equities compared to gilts, our advisers caution that having a high proportion of equities may expose us to the Regulator's scrutiny. According to their best practice, we should divert more of our fund into gilts. While this may reduce risk, it would also curtail our returns and limit future surpluses.

The Pension Protection Fund (PPF), established to safeguard scheme members when host companies face insolvency, now manages a staggering £39 billion on behalf of 295,000 members, including former employees of companies like Carillion. While the PPF has been successful in its mission, it, like many government initiatives, relies too heavily on algorithms rather than common sense.

Unfortunately, the rules governing the PPF do not cater to businesses that fall outside the mainstream, often leading to automated responses that spell 'No'. This is particularly true for the PPF, which insists that we pay a substantial levy each year to support schemes that have gone bankrupt. It feels like settling the restaurant bill for a table that has just run out without paying.

The most vexing aspect of this levy is its calculation, which hinges on two factors. The first factor, accounting for 20 per cent of the total, is the size of our scheme – a reasonable criterion. However, the remainder of the levy is determined by a risk-based calculation. Essentially, the more the computer perceives your company as likely to go under, the more it charges you. There are ten risk levels, with level 1 being the most desirable as it incurs the lowest fees.

The best we have ever achieved is level 2, which meant last year we paid £130,000. Strangely, we couldn't attain the coveted level 1 without resorting to borrowing money. The Pension Protection Fund's algorithm inexplicably suggests that having some debt makes a company less risky. It leaves one wondering, how can increasing debt reduce the likelihood of bankruptcy?

While we are frustrated that we can't reach level 1, I take solace in the fact that we entered the Covid pandemic with a healthy cash reserve and no debt. Had we been in debt two years ago, we would have struggled to maintain our commitment to paying our furloughed colleagues 100 per cent of their wages throughout the period when our shops were closed. We also continued to fulfill our obligations to landlords and suppliers. It was a conscious choice to be in band 2 to ensure our survival during the crisis, but as a consequence of doing the right thing, we then found ourselves in band 8!

When Prime Minister Boris Johnson instructed us all to stay at home and close our shops on March 23rd 2020, we followed the advice diligently. Our sales plummeted to zero, and we incurred losses of £1 million a week, but we managed to avoid going into an overdraft (though it was a close call).

The Pension Protection Fund's current calculations rely on our financial performance from that difficult period that, by any measure, was challenging for all businesses. When your sales plummet by 90 per cent because the law mandates the closure of your shops, no financial indicators appear favourable. I can understand why the Fund's statistical model, designed to predict insolvency, raised alarm bells.

However, perhaps it's time for the Fund to consider not only what the algorithm says but also how the business has performed in calmer seas. Our sales have surpassed pre-Covid levels, we've accumulated record levels of cash in the bank, we're opening new shops, and we've granted all our colleagues big pay increases. This doesn't resemble the behaviour of a failing business but rather that of a healthy one with minimal risk to the Fund.

The additional £230,000 we are now required to pay into the Levy due to our classification in band 8 could be better allocated to investments that would benefit our pensioners in their retirement. Alternatively, it could fund staff at the Fund and the Regulator to engage with businesses in person rather than relying solely on a model that often fails to comprehend how companies like ours truly operate. They might be astonished to discover that their computer doesn't always get it right.

What Have We Learned?

Treat suppliers fairly

Government policies should emphasize treating suppliers fairly. This can involve regulating relationships between large retailers and small, local suppliers, ensuring fair payment terms, and preventing monopolistic behaviour that can harm smaller businesses.

Landlords' role

Landlords play a critical role on the high street. The Government should encourage landlords to understand the needs of their tenants, such as local businesses and independent shops, and offer flexible leasing arrangements when appropriate.

Unintended consequences

Government intervention often brings unintended consequences. Regulations or tax policies aimed at revitalizing high streets may inadvertently burden businesses with excessive paperwork or costs. Constant evaluation and adjustment is needed to address these issues and ensure that policies are effective.

Adaptation for the future

High streets can have a strong future if they remain adaptable. The Government can support this by fostering innovation, providing grants or incentives for businesses to embrace technology, and creating spaces for cultural and community events to attract foot traffic.

Community and identity

High streets are more than just commercial spaces; they are integral parts of our communities and local identities. Government policies should reflect this by investing in infrastructure, promoting local events, and preserving historic or cultural landmarks on the high street.

SUCCESSION PLANNING AND THE FUTURE OF YOUR BUSINESS

Welcome to **Lesson Five,** where we will be looking ahead to the future for your organization. In this lesson, we dive into the world of effective succession planning and talent management. These aspects are crucial for ensuring the long-term success and sustainability of any organization, and in my book this needs to be the focus for any leader.

When running a company, succession planning goes beyond just filling key positions; it's about cultivating a pipeline of leaders who can steer the ship when needed. This connects us back to the foundations of setting up a company that we covered in **Lesson One** (page 13). We'll explore strategies to identify and nurture this future leadership talent within your organization, and in doing so ensure that your culture keeps getting stronger and people stay with you longer.

But what about the intersection of private equity investments and succession planning? We'll unravel the complexities, understanding how these investments can be both a bonus and a challenge. Learn how to navigate this terrain, ensuring financial growth while also preserving the values and culture that is key to your business. You *can* have one with the other.

Recognizing hidden talent within your workforce is an art in and of itself. We have already learned the best ways to be proactive in building a great team, fostering a great company culture, and looking outside of your immediate business to see what the competition are doing, in order to employ some of their initiatives and practices at your own. The best ideas are often close by, if you take the time to look. By identifying and developing the skills and abilities of your current team, you will find that, generally speaking, you will have a more engaged and productive one.

We'll delve into the debate surrounding remote work versus the traditional office environment, emphasizing the importance of a collaborative culture that not only supports colleagues but also complements your succession planning endeavours.

Finally, we'll explore the profound relationship between organisational culture and talent. A vibrant and inclusive culture can act as a catalyst for talent development, providing the fertile ground where future leaders can thrive. The more diverse your cohort, the better it performs.

Throughout this lesson, you will gain invaluable insights into the multifaceted world of succession planning and talent management. These are the cornerstones of a resilient and forward-looking organization. So, let's embark on this journey together, and equip you with the knowledge and strategies to navigate this critical aspect of modern business successfully.

PRIVATE EQUITY: WOULD THEIR GRANDCHILDREN BE PROUD?

The private equity market has long grappled with a public relations problem. Memories of past excesses and corporate raiding linger in the collective consciousness. However, the industry contends that it has evolved into a powerhouse of growth for the UK economy. The benefits of this growth need to be weighed against its broader impact, especially in terms of the tax revenue collected by His Majesty's Revenue and Customs (HMRC).

Addressing this perception problem is crucial, given the current trajectory of private equity (PE) activity. If this pace continues, a significant proportion of the UK's workforce may find themselves under the stewardship of a PE-owned company, so it's worth understanding how it works.

Over the last two decades, PE funds have witnessed exponential growth. They've become major players in the acquisition game, swallowing some of the UK's largest public and private companies. At times, this surge in corporate activity resembles a feeding frenzy. PE offers have frequently outperformed competing bids, whether from trade buyers or in public markets. As a result, founders often succumb to their allure and sell their businesses, while others opt for trade sales, initial public offerings (IPOs), or, in some cases, pass the baton to the next generation of their family to run the company.

While some notorious examples like Comet and Southern Cross have exposed the darker side of PE ownership, there are also instances where the industry has brought about positive transformations in companies, benefiting not only investors but also thousands of employees. The Hut Group, an online health and beauty business headquartered in Manchester, serves as a shining example. Their remarkable, albeit bumpy journey involved securing multiple rounds of private investment before successfully going public via an IPO. Notably, original investors like Balderton Capital in 2010 remain significant shareholders to this day.

Insights from individuals who have worked closely with PE companies suggest that, if approached with eyes wide open, the experience can be remarkably positive and profitable. Substantial wealth can be amassed in a relatively short period. However, PE firms are known for their sharp focus on returns, which can sometimes lead to misaligned interests, particularly when pension funds, upon which many rely, are among their investors.

My approach to running our business stands in stark contrast to standard PE operations. PE firms are known for their discipline, rationality, and relentless pursuit of growth, often through financial engineering. They specialize in strategies that involve leveraging debt to supercharge a company's growth potential. This approach, while effective, isn't always embraced by founders who might be uncomfortable with the idea of loading their companies with debt. In doing so, they may miss out on numerous opportunities for expansion. PE thrives in a competitive and often cyclical market, aiming to generate substantial returns for their investors, and they do this by using debt.

However, once a founder signs on the dotted line, everything changes. Investors come with a well-defined plan, which typically involves selling the business within 4–6 years, ideally at a profit surpassing their initial investment. If the management team remains onboard and excels, they stand to receive lucrative incentives that can be truly life changing.

While financial gain is a primary motivator, successful teams understand that running a business effectively, recruiting and inspiring top-tier talent, and timing their exit strategy correctly are the essential components of their journey.

The primary routes to growth often revolve around financial engineering. Taking on substantial debt, which subsequently reduces the company's taxable profits and, by extension, its corporate tax contributions, provides the necessary cash flow to fuel expansion. However, this approach comes with inherent risks. Plans can go awry, especially if the founder, who stays on to secure a substantial earn-out, hasn't fully grasped the intricacies of the deal or how PE truly operates.

Selecting the wrong PE partner can quickly strain relationships within a company. Regardless of size or complexity, businesses depend on successful relationships. Control rights clauses, for instance, can allow PE investors to exert significant influence, even if a founder retains the majority of shares, leading to potential conflicts. They say that even if you sell 1 per cent to PE, they can have effectively total control. Some retailers have suffered under PE ownership, particularly when valuable property assets are divested – as we are seeing with Morrisons supermarkets now – leaving the company burdened with high rents on long leases. The saga of Debenhams continues to cast a shadow over our high streets today.

As the PE industry continues to expand its footprint in corporate Britain, scrutiny will intensify. Questions will arise concerning the level of risk and the resulting profit when up to 70 per cent of a company may in effect be owned by banks rather than the PE firms themselves. Would greater alignment of interests reduce risk? If the tax regime underwent changes, requiring UK-based companies operating out of tax havens like the Cayman Islands or Luxembourg to pay their full income tax in the UK, would this impact the flow of funds into these structures in the future?

In my opinion, the best course of action for PE firms is to not only focus on financial outcomes but also run their companies with a strong emphasis on employee development and nurturing positive corporate cultures. Leaving a lasting and positive legacy can allow them to proudly recount their professional journey to their grandchildren in retirement. This approach not only benefits the firms themselves but also contributes positively to the broader business landscape, and the well-being of their employees and stakeholders.

Positive and Negative Aspects of Private Equity Investment:

Companies often find themselves at a crossroads when considering private equity (PE) investment. On one hand, there are compelling reasons to partner with PE firms, while on the other, there are potential downsides that must be navigated. Here are some key points to consider when weighing the pros and cons of a PE investor:

Positive Aspects

Access to capital

PE firms bring substantial financial resources, allowing companies to undertake ambitious growth strategies, make strategic acquisitions, or invest in research and development.

Operational expertize

PE investors typically have deep industry knowledge and a proven track record of operational improvement. They can provide valuable guidance on streamlining operations and increasing efficiency.

Network and contacts

PE firms often have extensive networks that can be leveraged for business development, partnerships, and market expansion.

Long-term vision

While PE firms aim for profitable exits, they also focus on building long-term value. This can align with the interests of the company's founders and management.

Negative Aspects

Short-term focus

PE firms typically have a defined investment horizon, which can lead to pressure on management to deliver quick results, potentially sacrificing long-term sustainability for short-term gains.

High debt levels

PE deals often involve leveraging the company with debt to fund growth or payouts to investors. This can increase financial risk and limit flexibility.

Loss of control

Founders and management may cede significant control to the PE investors, potentially affecting decision-making autonomy.

Exit strategy

PE investors have an exit plan from the beginning, which may not align with the company's preferred timeline or vision.

Now, let's delve deeper into how companies can navigate these aspects and maximize the benefits while minimizing the drawbacks of PE investments.

Strategies for Navigating PE Investment

Alignment of interests

Ensure that the goals and objectives of the company align with those of the PE firm. Clearly define expectations and strategies for value creation.

Effective communication

Maintain open and transparent communication between company leadership and PE investors. Regular updates and discussions can help avoid surprises.

Diversification of capital sources

Avoid overreliance on PE funding by diversifying capital sources. Explore alternative financing options to reduce debt levels and associated risks. Sometimes just taking your time and grinding it out is the best strategy.

Risk mitigation

Develop risk mitigation strategies to handle potential downsides, such as contingency plans for adverse market conditions.

Talent retention

Identify key individuals within the organization who can drive change and lead the company through the transition. Implement retention strategies to keep these individuals engaged.

Valuable lessons can often be gleaned from seemingly unrelated fields.

IDENTIFYING SUCCESSION PLANNING CANDIDATES

Succession planning is crucial but often overlooked for companies, especially when navigating changes brought about by PE investment. Here are ways to identify individuals within the company who can play pivotal roles in succession planning:

Leadership potential
Assess colleagues for leadership qualities, including communication skills, problem-solving abilities, and adaptability. Look for individuals who can step into senior leadership roles, even if they are five years off this level of responsibility.

Industry knowledge
Identify colleagues with deep industry knowledge and expertize, as they can help guide the company through industry-specific challenges. People who've 'been there before' are a safer bet than those who haven't.

Adaptability
Seek individuals who are open to change and can adapt to new strategies and corporate cultures. Resilience and flexibility are valuable traits during transitions.

Mentoring skills
Employees who excel in mentoring and coaching can play essential roles in developing the next generation of leaders within the company.

Commitment

Look for employees who are committed to the company's long-term success and share its core values. Job hoppers aren't helpful. These individuals are more likely to invest their energy in ensuring a smooth transition during PE ownership.

FINDING A SUCCESSOR AMONG THE TEAM

Valuable lessons can often be gleaned from seemingly unrelated fields, and one such domain is the management of talent. While we typically associate the recruitment and development of talent with the corporate sphere, it's worth looking at how other sectors, such as professional sports, excel in this aspect.

Let's take football clubs, for instance. Beyond their ability to inspire ardent fan bases and secure lucrative television deals, they excel in managing talent and succession planning, setting a noteworthy example for the business world.

Consider the case of Phil Foden, the 23-year-old midfielder for Manchester City. Foden's journey with the club began at the tender age of four, and he has since emerged as one of the world's most valuable football players. The exceptional talent displayed by Foden was not only recognized by the coaches but also by the club's owners. They understood the financial wisdom in nurturing homegrown talent rather than solely relying on external acquisitions. Additionally, Manchester City's unique culture and history become ingrained in this young talent from an early age, ensuring a seamless transition into the first team.

Interestingly, the world of football management often diverges from this approach. Take, for instance, the transition from Sir Alex Ferguson to David Moyes at Manchester United. This move resulted in a sharp decline in the club's value and on-pitch performance. While Moyes was highly regarded, the change didn't yield the intended results. This example illustrates the potential risks associated with bringing in external talent, even when they come with stellar reputations. Similar scenarios frequently unfold in the business world. ⁎

Succession planning, sometimes referred to as talent management by HR professionals, has emerged as one of the most critical risk management processes for companies, and this means companies of all sizes. In reality if you employ only one person, you need a succession plan. Yet, many organizations shy away from it. In cases where it is executed effectively, typically within larger firms, future stars are not only identified but also developed, reducing the reliance on external specialists. Moreover, effective succession planning saves substantial amounts of money.

A friend who specializes in executive recruitment recently confided that if the companies he collaborates with made more of an effort in their own succession planning efforts, he would stand to lose 80 per cent of his business.

At Timpson, a small group meets every three months to review succession planning. Their overarching goal is to identify and nurture two potential superstars for each role, while providing necessary training and support along the way. In some instances, when roles are highly specialized, external searches are necessary. In such cases, it's viewed as a failure on the organization's part for not cultivating internal talent sooner, and therefore costing us a headhunter's fee that needs to be paid. The key lesson here is that identifying potential successors should ideally begin as soon as an individual assumes a role within the company.

One of the more enjoyable aspects of succession planning is presenting future stars with challenges to assess how good they really are. In the context of Timpson's business, this often involves working in retail shops, supporting area teams, and undertaking small projects such as researching potential business acquisitions. While some individuals thrive under such challenges, others find themselves out of their depth.

It's worth noting that managers and team leaders have a tendency to over-promote individuals, attributing this to the organization's desire to encourage personal growth and ambition. This approach is intended to serve as a test, an inspiration, and an opportunity for individuals to explore their potential within the company. However, when things go awry, it's a situation that needs swift correction. It's not the individual's fault they have failed in the more senior role, but the fault of the leaders who have promoted them too early. The most concerning scenario is when such issues arise at the level of the new CEO.

Harvard Business School conducted a study on recruitment, revealing that external CEO appointments tend to yield positive results primarily when a company is in dire straits. These external CEOs are often brought in to effect changes in failing corporate cultures and strategies, and their efforts are rewarded with substantial bonuses. Conversely, when a company is performing well and an external CEO is appointed, it frequently leads to the destruction of significant shareholder value. Moreover, external CEOs typically receive salaries that are, on average, 15 per cent higher than those of internally promoted candidates. While these appointments may benefit the recruitment industry, they don't necessarily translate to favourable outcomes for shareholders.

Family businesses, in particular, grapple with distinct challenges related to succession planning. Balancing the inspiration and development of non-family colleagues, while grooming family members who are eager to join the business, is a delicate endeavour.

The television series *Succession*, a satirical take on the dysfunctional Roy family's business empire, provides a glimpse into the extremes that family-run enterprises can encounter. The patriarch, Logan Roy, experiencing declining health, has his four children battle for prominence and – ultimately – control in the company, leading to internal power struggles. While the series is far from reality, it does underscore the challenges involved in managing family succession for businesses that are family-owned.

In many cases, the most capable individuals within a company are not necessarily those related to the owner or founder. The argument can be made that everyone should be treated as equals, regardless of their last name. Promotions should ideally be based on merit rather than lineage. When I joined our family business in 1995 as a shop colleague, one of our non-executive directors assumed the role of overseeing my career progression within the company. This arrangement proved beneficial, as it was more straightforward for someone other than my dad to engage in potentially difficult conversations about my professional development. Evidently, I passed muster, as my responsibilities increased over time. I began identifying my strengths and areas where I could make the most significant contributions, and what areas I should stay well away from. This experience underscored to me the importance of effective succession management.

Mars, a vast private business that has remained in the family for five generations, offers a textbook example of how astute succession planning can benefit all stakeholders within the company. Forrest Mars, who had a complex relationship with his father, founded a confectionery and pet food business in Europe. Upon his father's death in 1934, he merged his venture with the family business, embarking on a mission to develop a robust succession plan to avoid the challenges he faced as a younger man. At the age of 69, Forrest Mars retired and entrusted the reins of the company to his four children. Their role as owners was to serve as stewards of succession management, by identifying the most promising young colleagues and facilitating their growth. This approach has undoubtedly paid off.

On reflection, it's evident that the journey to leadership and success typically involves hard work, dedication, and fair amounts of luck. However, equally important are the kindness and foresight of others. Regrettably, countless talented individuals never receive the opportunities they deserve simply because they go unnoticed. It is incumbent upon those of us in positions of power to identify these future stars, and derive satisfaction from watching them thrive. This is where true leadership lies – recognizing potential and nurturing it to fruition.

As leaders, we must embrace the responsibility of recognizing and nurturing talent within our ranks. By doing so, we not only secure the future success of our organizations but also contribute to the personal growth and development of individuals who may otherwise remain hidden gems.

One of the key takeaways from examining the success of football clubs in talent management is the significance of early identification and development. In the corporate world, this translates to the importance of recognizing potential talent at the earliest stages of an individual's career within the organization.

The success of football clubs in managing talent and planning for succession provides valuable insights for the corporate world. Identifying and nurturing talent from within, as exemplified by Manchester City's Phil Foden, can yield exceptional results. However, it's crucial to recognize the potential risks associated with bringing in external talent, as demonstrated by the example of Manchester United. For clarity and openness, I support Manchester City!

THE IMPORTANCE OF RETURNING TO THE OFFICE: FOSTERING A CULTURE OF SUCCESS

The concept of working from home has gained momentum, with many hailing it as the future of work. While remote work undoubtedly offers flexibility and convenience, there's a growing recognition of its limitations, particularly concerning career progression, social interaction, and mental health. I truly believe in the value of returning to the office, surrounded by a work culture that supports colleagues and prioritizes their wellbeing. This approach not only aligns with succession planning but also fosters an environment where colleagues can excel and be promoted based on their capabilities, skills, and work commitment. I doubt someone would be promoted if they rarely went to the office, and didn't get face time with their peers.

The lost sense of community in remote work

For many, working from home is a privilege rather than an entitlement. While it may seem like a boon, the reality is that remote work can lead to feelings of isolation, hinder career growth, and negatively impact mental health. Employees spending their days alone at home are more likely to miss out on promotions and the sense of belonging that comes from being part of a vibrant workplace community.

The resurgence of in-person work

The tide is beginning to turn, as evidenced by the increasing number of people returning to their workplaces. The initial allure of remote work is giving way to the recognition that being together in a work community has unique advantages. It's crucial not to let the preferences of a small minority who benefit from remote work overshadow the benefits of in-person collaboration. I haven't yet met a CEO who doesn't want everyone back in the office five days a week.

Understanding employee preferences

A colleague survey conducted at a Canary Wharf-based firm revealed a telling insight: people's social lives were the primary motivator for coming to the office, not necessarily the company's success. Thursday emerged as the most popular day for in-person work, likely due to it being 'beer night' in London. Conversely, Fridays and Wednesdays were the days people preferred off. This suggests that the most productive workdays were potentially limited to Mondays and Tuesdays.

The short-term benefits of remote work

While there are undoubtedly short-term benefits to remote work, such as cost savings on commuting and a reduced carbon footprint, these advantages may come at a long-term cost to the individual. The ability to network, get promoted, and engage in vital activities like troubleshooting and discussing strategy plans are compromised when colleagues are isolated. Solving problems and contributing to the company's success often requires a physical presence.

The dangers of a solely remote workforce

Many companies have realized significant savings through remote work, particularly in terms of travel expenses and office rents. However, these cost savings can come at a significant price. Without a vibrant office culture and an inspiring work environment, attracting top talent becomes challenging. When pay is the only differentiator, it's difficult to compete effectively in the job market.

The benefits of an in-person work environment

At Timpson, the office reopened to all colleagues after the Covid lockdowns, aligning with the reopening of the shops. The decision was rooted in the belief that colleagues and customers are best served when we are all working together.

The improved pace, innovative exchange of ideas, and overall performance of the business were noticeable when everyone returned to work after lockdowns. We also were better equipped to spot colleagues who were having problems away from work, and challenge the odd 'work shy' colleague. This experience underscores my view that having everyone back in the office is good for business.

The importance of company culture

Every company's culture is unique, shaped by its history, people, and sense of identity. When a significant portion of colleagues operates remotely, there's a risk that the company's culture will be diluted and become indistinguishable from others. Strong cultures with personal bonds among colleagues mean companies are better equipped to face challenges and stand out in the market.

The role of technology in the office

While tools like Zoom and Teams were indispensable during lockdowns, they have limitations in facilitating effective communication. In-person meetings allow for better decision-making, by enabling participants to gauge body language and ensure everyone is engaged in the conversation. Virtual meeting platforms remain useful tools, but they are not a substitute for the dynamism of face-to-face interactions.

Hybrid models: balancing flexibility and commitment

Nici Bush, Vice President of Workplace Transformation at Mars, suggests that traditional fixed hours are becoming obsolete, and a hybrid work model is the way forward. While this approach works well for many, it's essential to acknowledge that some professions require specific working hours to deliver services effectively. Employees in such roles may not have the luxury of choosing when and how they work. Someone has to stock the shelves overnight for customers arriving the next day . . .

The message is clear: return to the office
The message is unequivocal: if you aspire to earn promotions, increase your income, and enjoy a fulfilling work experience, it's time to return to the office. Remote work offers convenience, but it often falls short in terms of career growth, social interaction, and mental wellbeing for new members of the team. By fostering a culture that prioritizes collaboration, mentorship, and employee support, all covered in **Lesson Two** (page 47), companies can create an environment where colleagues can thrive and, in turn, contribute to the organization's success. The office is more than a physical space; it's a hub of innovation, growth, and camaraderie that propels individuals toward their career goals.

NOT EVERY BUSINESS IS THE SAME: FINDING BALANCE IN A REMOTE WORLD

While the traditional office set-up has long stood as the bedrock of our company, and because we ask that every single member of the wider team be in the office due to our colleagues serving the community, it is important to remember that not every business can operate in the same way that we do.

The benefits of being in the office, particularly for our business, are clear and allows us to fully connect with the people we work with daily, which results in a faster response rate should a problem need solving or an innovative idea that we are keen to see implemented avoid becoming stalled due to any approval processes. Obviously, sometimes, there are situations where we are more flexible, especially if any of our colleagues have gone through a difficult situation – in or out of work – we would investigate a phased return to the office so that they could manage their duties with the support of their managers and the wider team. This is also a standard practice when any of our colleagues are experiencing health issues that affect their working lives.

As we are a retail company, remote working simply does not work for our business as most of our colleagues are serving the people that pay our wages, or are supplying the materials that those members of the team need directly from the warehouse. We operate with a blanket policy that is fair to every member of the team, which is to say: if the people on the shop floor and in the warehouse are in each day, so should the people at the office. However, I am aware that for some industries, particularly those operating outside of retail or hospitality, that this five-day work week would be unsuited for their operations or unsustainable for them and their colleagues. This is especially apparent in companies and industries working across multiple time zones or continents.

The workplace is a continually changing landscape and the traditional 9-to-5 model may not be suitable for everyone in modern-day work dynamics. Today, there often needs to be a more nuanced understanding of your colleagues and the company, its needs and whether you have the technology and abilities to action the change while, crucially, ensuring that it does not detract or move too far away from the wider needs of your business and the brilliant team that you work with.

Remote work took off in a big way when everyone in the world, frankly, had to adapt to changing circumstances in response to a global pandemic. However, even before this was the case, many companies had started hiring remote-access and flexible colleagues. Tim Ferris, the author of *Tools of Titans* and *The 4-Hour Work Week*, advocates for hiring remote workers or virtual assistants as it gives leaders and those managing teams the freedom to focus on more crucial and important tasks. Aside from its benefits for leaders, there are also other factors that have seen a vast improvement in individuals' work-life balance.

The convenience it offers extends beyond the professional sphere, touching on aspects such as diminished commuting strain, freedom for parents to share or more easily manage childcare, and cost savings.

Merit-based recognition over physical presence
Challenging the conventional belief that promotions hinge on physical office presence is, for some, a perspective that needs to be more widespread. Remote work provides a platform for individuals to showcase their capabilities and dedication through measurable achievements, which move beyond the superficiality of simply being in the office. Shifting the focus from face-to-face time to tangible outcomes cultivates a culture

that places genuine value on results rather than conformity to office norms.

The long-term potential of remote work

Valid concerns surrounding career growth and social interaction in remote settings are the most prevalent issues raised by employers and businesses. However, just as with fostering a great company culture in the office, there are also ways to build this into your virtual workplace, which can cut down on email traffic and allow colleagues to collaborate in and out of working hours, while also allowing them to focus on larger, more detail-intensive projects. If your company is international and your team are spread across different time zones, ensuring that the online meetings foster a network of support to any new members of the team by taking a welcome call with everyone they'll be working with or by actioning break-out meetings with specific members of the team, you may find that some colleagues perform better than they typically would in a physical location.

Safeguarding work-life harmony and mental wellbeing

Although there are cases where isolation and compromised mental health do affect those working remotely, a great number of people entering the workforce today have had access to the internet throughout their entire lives and are much more tech-savvy, which can allow them to perform tasks more efficiently, with greater ease and full autonomy from the comfort of their homes. If this is a real concern to you or your business, it is a good idea to offer support structures like a go-to 'buddy' they can meet with for regular check-ins to ensure that anybody working remotely has the same benefits, support network and access that puts employee wellbeing first. If you can have a blend of office and working days, this will also help counterbalance these concerns.

Strategic economics: unlocking cost-efficiency and attracting top talent
Remote work can also lead to cost savings, benefiting both organizations and colleagues alike. By shifting resources from the renting of traditional office spaces towards compensation packages can not only help save you money but also acts as an attractive working solution to potential team members who may, for whatever reason, be unable to work in the office five days a week. Or, which can often be the case during contract negotiation, when the best person for the job can only work a select number of days due to personal commitments, or previous benefits at another company, but comes highly recommended and consistently delivers then letting them work in a way that works best for them and yields results for the company can't be a bad thing now, can it?

Embracing hybrid models
While advocating for a complete return to the office is the right approach for many companies, embracing a hybrid-working model of perhaps three days in the office and two days remotely can also lead to a more diverse pool of colleagues. Hybrid models strike a delicate balance, recognizing the advantages of in-person collaboration while preserving flexibility for roles or duties that thrive in remote settings. This balance between adaptability and commitment ensures that each team member can contribute effectively, irrespective of their physical location.

What Have We Learned?

The power of forward thinking
Lesson Five has illuminated the significance of looking ahead in the world of business. By embracing change, adapting to new technologies, and forecasting market trends, companies can position themselves for sustained success.

Strategic planning is paramount
We've discovered that strategic planning is not just a buzzword but a critical aspect of thriving in business today. Setting clear goals, aligning resources, and consistently evaluating your strategies can make all the difference.

Innovation as a driver
Lesson Five underscores the role of innovation as a driving force for any enterprise. Being open to fresh ideas, fostering a culture of creativity, and daring to innovate can propel a company to new heights.

Adaptability in action
We've learned that adaptability is not just about surviving but thriving in a constantly changing world. Companies that can pivot quickly, learn from challenges, and stay agile are better equipped to navigate the uncertain road ahead.

The human element
Finally, we've seen that amidst technological advancements, the human element remains at the heart of every successful business. Nurturing talent, fostering teamwork, and caring for employee wellbeing are keys to achieving sustainable growth.

LESSON SIX

LEAD BY EXAMPLE

Welcome to **Lesson Six**, where we delve into the pivotal aspects of leadership within the context of the broader journey we've been on. In the previous lessons, we've explored building a thriving company culture, prioritizing colleague wellbeing, fostering a strong outward perspective to the world, and considering the influence of external factors on our business. Now, we turn our attention to the driving force that brings these elements together: effective leadership.

Throughout this lesson, you will gain insights into the critical role of leadership in not only shaping company culture, but also in fostering colleague wellbeing, and enabling your business to thrive in an ever-changing world.

Effective leadership is the cornerstone on which all successful organizations are built. It's the glue that holds together the various facets we've explored in previous lessons. A great leader not only sets the tone for the company culture but also champions the wellbeing of everyone who works and depends on the company's success, ensuring they are motivated and fulfilled in their roles.

This lesson will provide you with practical guidance and real-world examples that illustrate the value of leadership within an organization. You will learn about creating a work environment where leadership doesn't just come from the top but is encouraged at all levels, empowering your team members to excel and contribute to the company's success.

We will also discuss the importance of kindness and humility in leadership, demonstrating how these qualities enhance overall performance and employee happiness.

Finally, we will explore how a leader's skills and qualities are instrumental in guiding a company through times of change and challenge, both on a micro and macro level. I must point out that I have had many failings along my leadership journey, but these lessons have helped me be a better boss along the way, and I hope they help you too.

So, as we embark on **Lesson Six**, remember that leadership is not confined to a particular role or title within the organization. It's a collective effort that influences company culture, colleague wellbeing, and the company's success in the global context. Let's explore the principles, practices, and qualities that define effective leadership, and learn how they tie together the lessons from our journey thus far.

LANGUAGE MATTERS

The way we speak at work matters more than you might realize at first.

Every company has its own unique language, a set of jargon, job titles, and acronyms that can turn newcomers' heads and leave them bewildered. It's a rite of passage to decode this cryptic language, but it doesn't always have to be this way.

Language is a powerful tool that shapes our culture and values. At Timpson we do things a bit differently and refuse to play the jargon game that leaves people feeling left out and confused (see page 181). Instead, we've embraced a different way – one in which we hope inclusivity reigns supreme in everything we do.

Titles that empower

Job titles may seem inconsequential, but they wield immense influence over our self-perception, and the value we bring to our roles. In many companies, you might be labeled a staff member, a team member, an employee, or a colleague. The words used may appear trivial, but they can profoundly affect how we view our jobs. At Timpson, we've adopted the title 'colleague' because it reflects our belief that no one is superior to another. Here, it doesn't matter what your paycheck looks like or what your business card says; everyone is simply a colleague.

Within Timpson, we've created a culture where titles are designed to empower. We have the Director of Happiness, the Financial First Aider, and the Mental Health Specialist, all working to make each colleague feel valued and supported.

Our Directors of Smiles, Paul and Lauren, remind everyone who steps into Timpson House that a warm welcome is at the heart of our operation.

Elon Musk, the iconic entrepreneur behind Tesla, has taken an unconventional approach to job titles. He now goes by the title Technoking of Tesla, and his CFO is known as the Master of Coin. These titles may seem eccentric, but they encapsulate the uniqueness and innovation that Tesla represents. While we might not have ventured to such extremes, we have our HR Director Gouy, affectionately known as the Director of Colleague Support, and Duke the office dog, who carries the job title Head of Entertainment. These titles aren't just whimsical; they serve as a constant reminder of the warmth and hospitality that defines our company.

But we don't stop at predefined titles. At Timpson, we encourage our colleagues to get creative and design their own job titles, reflecting their personalities and roles. While some may push the boundaries, we welcome their enthusiasm, and ensure they are content with what's on their business cards. I'll admit, even I am uncomfortable with my own title as Chief Executive, which feels a bit corporate and, well, a tad dull. However, I'm not quite prepared to fully embrace the Elon Musk school of thought just yet.

The significance of names

In the world of business, even something as seemingly simple as a name carries profound significance. It's not just a sequence of letters; it's a symbol of identity and belonging. Let me share a story that highlights the importance of this, in the context of Timpson's ethos.

When my father joined our family business back in the late 1960s, he was politely addressed as 'Mr John'. Fast forward to today, and he is content with simply being called 'John'. The shift from a formal title to a first name is more than just semantics; it reflects a fundamental shift in our company culture.

At Timpson, we embrace informality and camaraderie. We address each other by our first names, or even playful nicknames. To ensure we get it right, we maintain a 'known as' list. When a new colleague joins, it's not only about knowing their full name; it's about understanding what they prefer to be called. A simple 'Michael' could be a 'Mick', a 'Mike', or even a 'Mikey'. It may seem like a trivial detail, but it's essential to get it right when we reach out to someone. It's a small gesture that signifies respect, and creates a profound sense of belonging in our workplace.

And then, there's Senga. Her real name is Agnes, but she chooses to stand out at work by using her name spelled backwards. This is a powerful statement, reflecting the freedom and flexibility we grant our colleagues to be their authentic selves. Getting someone's name right might seem inconsequential, but it holds the same weight as ensuring their paycheck is accurate. It's a mark of respect and acknowledgment that every individual, regardless of their role, is an integral part of our Timpson family.

This practice of addressing each other by our preferred names isn't just a superficial change. It underscores our commitment to creating an inclusive environment where people feel valued, seen, and heard. It's an extension of our belief that everyone, from the CEO to the newest recruit, has a vital role to play and a unique identity to celebrate. Just as we encourage colleagues to choose their own job titles, we also encourage them to define their own identities within the Timpson family. This ethos is woven into the fabric of our company culture, where language is not a barrier but a bridge to stronger connections and a more inclusive workplace.

The art of saying 'no'

In reality, the job of leading a company isn't as glamorous as some people think when they first imagine what goes on from day to day. Yes, it's great to be your own boss, but with responsibility comes a long list of jobs that no one else really can do or, importantly, wants to do. When you're responsible for thousands of colleagues, and in turn their families' livelihoods, you know you've got to get it right, and to ensure that the company is financially safe, in combination with making sure that your colleagues are well looked after.

Instead of spending my time sitting in meetings where we discuss the design of the latest shop fit, or creating a new service to add to our shops, most of my time is spent visiting shops, and saying 'no'. In my book, a leader's job is to say 'no' to at least 95 per cent of the ideas that are pitched to you.

This isn't because they are bad ideas, it's because they add complexity and don't move the dial, and this in turn can impact our well-established company culture. We want to run a simple business where our culture is nurtured not damaged, and from experience adding in a constant stream of new ideas detracts from our customer offer and increases costs.

An interesting comparison is Sainsbury's and B&M, both FTSE 100 retail companies that are worth about the same amount of money. There is one big difference between them.

Sainsbury's employs five times as many people as B&M do, while making the same level of profit. This is because B&M has had a long-term policy of keeping things simple, and not adding in new products and services that add complexity. Sainsbury's, on the other hand, chase the last 3 per cent of sales. This last 3 per cent in theory should drop to the bottom line, but in reality, it requires extra overheads, warehouse space, and colleague time in store. When Tesco dropped 20 per cent of the products in its ranges, sales – along with profits – actually went up.

So, there is a good reason to say no to what seem like good ideas: they end up costing you money. Our way to drive more sales is to sell more of what we've got. Sometimes we add in a new service, but when I look back at when we tried spectacle repairs, and even selling leather belts, I shiver with shame as they never worked, and were never going to work. I should have been braver, and said no before we even took our first step.

As businesses mature more complexity creeps in. More reports are written, more meetings are held, and more processes initiated. To combat the insatiable desire of some people to want more and more analysis and structure, we set up the Cut the Crap Committee. It's run by Paresh our Financial Director and meets every three months to identify any unnecessary, costly processes and reports, and then bin them. The committee includes colleagues from all areas of the business and takes pride in extinguishing as many pointless things they can find.

Twice a year Paresh and I also go through a month's worth of invoices, to spot unnecessary costs, and products and services we never needed. It's a thankless task but we always find at least £50,000 of costs to be saved, and challenge suppliers to simplify their systems so we can be more efficient in paying them quickly.

So being across the detail brings its benefits to a leader, but it's a case of dipping in occasionally, and then making a hasty retreat. As I have said previously, leave the middle bit of the organization to the experts you have employed, and let them get on with the processes needed to support the front-line colleagues. But from time to time you need to look in and check the processes are essential, money isn't being wasted, and your practices are aligned with your core company values.

Language Builds Trust

When we acquired Snappy Snaps, a chain of 120 franchised photo shops, trust became our most precious currency. Many were sceptical about our ability to manage a franchised business, and rightly so as this was a first for us. There were problems to solve, some of them costly. However, the most critical change cost us nothing. Instead of labelling the shop owners as 'franchisees', we embraced the term 'partners'. This seemingly simple linguistic shift set the tone for our approach; we were in this together, committed to solving our problems collaboratively.

And we aren't alone in our commitment to inclusive language. Companies like Bruntwood, a commercial property business with offices across the UK, share our language ethos. They have replaced the term 'tenants' with 'customers'. This choice in language signifies the kind of company they are – one that places the customer at the heart of its operations. Other forward-thinking companies in the UK are also adopting similar approaches, recognizing that language plays a pivotal role in shaping company culture and relationships.

It's great to be your own boss, but with responsibility comes a long list of jobs that no one else really can do or, importantly, wants to do.

THE PITFALLS OF CORPORATE JARGON

Corporate jargon can be maddening. It tends to isolate those who aren't in the know, and make those who use it sound like they've walked straight out of a sitcom like *The Office*. It's almost like a trend, where people create their own secret language to fit into the start-up culture. But this trend has taken a turn for the worse, and the corporate world is swimming in a sea of jargon.

I found myself on a Zoom call not too long ago, advising a friend's son who was navigating the challenging world of a tech start-up. In just a few minutes, he unleashed a barrage of jargon, firmly anchoring himself in the start-up culture. These phrases – 'let's circle back', 'identifying pain points', 'trying to solve everything at once', 'clarifying responsibilities', and the rather ominous 'pushing the boundaries' – were like a foreign language to me. Suffice to say, I wasn't the best guide to help him find the 'magic solution'.

Corporate Jargon	Alternative Phrasing
Thinking outside the box	Seek innovative solutions
Synergy	Work together effectively
Drill down	Examine in detail
Best practices	Key strengths
Going forward	In-depth analysis
On the same page	In agreement
Buy-in	Gain support
Low-hanging fruit	Easy targets/quick wins
Core competencies	Key skills
Think outside the box	Be creative

Empower	Enable/strengthen
Run it up the flagpole	Test the waters
Actionable	Practical/feasible
Take it offline	Discuss it privately

Our company language is based on having adaptability at its core. We understand that effective communication means different things to different people. Whether we're dealing with wider teams, individuals, or third parties, we strive to use language that's inclusive, understandable, and effective. Sometimes people find it difficult to say the simple word of 'no'. It's about creating a workplace where people can be direct, feel heard, understood, and valued, and where language is a tool for collaboration, not a barrier.

THE IMPORTANCE OF HONESTY, OPEN COMMUNICATION, AND CLARITY IN TEAMWORK

Every Friday, I receive an email that lists the names of colleagues who have either joined or left our company during the week. The numbers fluctuate, but one unfortunate consistency is that we bid farewell to someone who has been dishonest. On average, this happens twice a week, and it's a painful reality we all regret.

In the world of Timpson, honesty is a bedrock principle, deeply rooted in our values. It all harks back to the very first day, with Timpson's two golden rules:

- Look the part.
- Put the money in the till.

Clear, direct, and unequivocal – these rules exemplify our commitment to straightforward language and conduct. They are the foundations upon which we build our relationships, both within the company and with our customers.

Most colleagues who break the first of these rules are granted a second, or even a third, chance to learn from their mistakes. In fact, many of them eventually evolve into great colleagues over time. But there comes a point when individuals cross a line that necessitates a difficult conversation – a conversation where they have to go home and tell their loved ones that they've been let go.

We acknowledge that not all dishonesty makes headline news. While the media often reports on large-scale corporate frauds, most dishonesty remains hidden beneath the surface, in the form of minor fiddles, wheezes, and scams. Timpson, too, has had its share of such incidents.

I have friends who run businesses and are seemingly obsessed with preventing themselves from being defrauded. They dedicate an inordinate amount of time to catching culprits and making examples out of them. In contrast, my focus is on inspiring the 99 per cent of colleagues who are honest. However, I must acknowledge that this is a problem we cannot entirely evade – it's the less glamorous side of leadership.

To tackle this issue, we employ an unconventional strategy: we share with our colleagues the most effective ways they could steal from us. It may sound counterintuitive, but by making it clear that we are aware of such practices, we reduce the likelihood of them occurring in the first place. After all, if you know there's a speed camera around the corner, you're less likely to speed. We publish an updated list every six months in our newsletter, detailing the reasons colleagues have been dismissed, and the actions that led to their dismissal. The top five reasons remain consistent, but new 'wheezes' or scams that we hadn't previously detected are sometimes added to the list.

One of my favourite examples is from a few years back when we introduced new tills into our shops. An enterprising colleague in one of our stores purchased a replica till from the same supplier. His till found its way into the shop and served customers for two years, while our official till sat in his living room. Every night, he entered fake transactions and submitted paperwork as if everything were normal. It was an audacious scam, but it wasn't sustainable. He eventually got married and had a dilemma. If he went on honeymoon, who would carry on the scam and keep raking off the proceeds into his pocket? His wife won the day and he had a lovely honeymoon, but in the shop the sales surged by 50 per cent and we then noticed a discrepancy in till numbers. His career was over. Though he managed to pocket a significant amount of money (tax-free), he lost his job and, ultimately, his new wife who was disgusted at his dishonesty.

Most dishonesty, however, occurs on a smaller scale but is no less significant. It ranges from stealing cash and stock to time theft and, increasingly, information theft. We are all vulnerable to colleagues who refuse to play by the rules. We may never know the full extent of what's taken from us, but I'm confident it amounts to millions every year.

I doubt colleagues join our company with theft in mind. Circumstances in their lives take unfortunate turns, and they perceive us as an easy solution to their immediate problems. Many theft problems arise from issues related to gambling, poor financial planning, or substance abuse. We can assist with all of these, provided we are aware of them. Hence, we foster a culture that encourages colleagues to come forward and seek help. We hate sacking people, but we love helping them.

Furthermore, we have implemented a support system to help colleagues navigate financial crises, and we hope it means they are less likely to put their hands in the till. While we're not a bank, we understand that short-term cash flow problems can tempt individuals to become a bad actor. In many cases, we lend money, or even provide financial advice, while helping them with financial planning. Most colleagues are skilled at budgeting, but unforeseen life events such as funeral expenses or a malfunctioning boiler can throw a wrench into their plans. This is where the support of a good company can make a difference. On average, each year the company pays for 8 funerals of colleagues' family members, as there are times when there are no funds to bury a loved one with dignity.

Dealing with issues related to drugs and gambling can be more complex, often arising from deep-rooted problems. These challenges aren't easily resolved. We provide referrals to addiction charities, and offer access to our full-time counsellor, Elaine. In these cases, the levels of debt can be staggering, physical health may be compromised, and long-term solutions are required. These colleagues are often exceptional at their jobs but require help to overcome their problems. When they do, it's a win-win situation – we have a happy, healthy colleague, and our sales go up.

It's well known that we recruit people from prison; individuals who have broken the law and failed society in the past. Ironically, these colleagues rarely have gross misconduct cases against their names. They seldom transgress. Their experience has taught them the significance of abiding by the rules. In essence, everyone deserves a second chance, and companies that recognize the challenges people face in their lives, fostering a culture of support, will ultimately have the best, most honest, workforce.

Here at Timpson, we are carving our own path. We are committed to nurturing talent, fostering inclusivity, and expressing gratitude. We've broken free from the conventional norms, creating a workplace where colleagues feel valued, understood, and empowered. The following pages will dive deeper into another corporate quagmire – the long and laborious company meetings that often offer little benefit.

Kindness comes from the top

Every so often at Timpson, we make the decision to promote a colleague into a senior leadership role. It's a pivotal moment for both the individual, their family, and the company. But let's be honest, no matter how skilled you are at spotting talent, it doesn't always unfold as expected. Overpromoting someone can be a harsh blow, and as the leader, it's your responsibility to resolve the situation you've inadvertently created. The key to doing this is through speed, kindness, and generosity.

I believe that it's vital to give new leaders the right advice, to set them on the path to success from day one. This is why

I write a heartfelt, handwritten letter offering my guidance. The most successful leaders are those who empower their team members to be the best versions of themselves – and it just so happens that these leaders are usually the ones who generate the most profit. To be a leader who is respected and admired, you must consistently get a few fundamental things right. These tips might seem obvious, but they're not typically part of a business school curriculum. They come from my own learnings through many mistakes and experiences.

In leadership, it's essential to understand that small things can have a massive impact on people. When your colleagues face issues like a delayed stock order, a malfunctioning printer, or missing overtime pay, it affects their morale and productivity. A great leader takes the time to discover what's going wrong on the front lines, and takes pride in resolving these issues. It's all about being attentive to the little details that matter to your team.

Some executives prefer spending their time in boardrooms, strategizing for the future, but the most effective leaders are those who know the intricate details of their operation, which is why it's so important to fully understand and see your business from the ground up. I've always believed that most meetings are a waste of time, whereas time spent on the front line is never squandered. I'm continually surprised by how little time some retail leaders spend in their shops, serving customers and contributing to the company's bottom line.

I tend to focus my time on visiting shops, talking to my colleagues who serve customers every day, and with the leaders of the company. I don't spend much time in the engine room of middle management. They have a job to do, and in my view are best left to get on with it. They have processes to carry out, decisions to make, and timescales to hit. In the past I've seen failing leaders focus far too much on this area, as it's easier. Fiddling around with the details makes you feel like you're busy, but I have learned instead that getting up early to see shops in far flung places, to learn what's going right and wrong, and being happy to be challenged by your directors are the places where you develop the business and make money.

Justin King, once CEO of Sainsbury's, bucked this trend of spending too much time in the boardroom. On his first day at the helm, he chose to spend his day in a warehouse instead of the head office where everyone was eagerly awaiting his arrival. This set the tone for his decade-long tenure at the company, focusing on rectifying the operational issues he inherited. After all, having a brilliant strategy means nothing if your merchandise isn't on the shelves.

If you were to ask any colleague at Richer Sounds, they'd confirm that their founder, Julian Richer, is a master of detail. He knows the sales breakdown for every shop each week, where issues have arisen, what suggestions have been put forward, and which colleagues are facing personal challenges. While it might not be the most glamorous aspect of leadership, it's undoubtedly the most effective way to boost profits, and show your colleagues that you genuinely care. It fosters a work environment where everyone strives to perform at their best.

Leadership is, in large part, about making decisions. Unfortunately, many people are hesitant to make decisions independently, relying on consultants, market research, and extensive data. I prefer my leaders to be self-assured in making

.

quick decisions based on their gut instincts, rather than being driven solely by data. The more you understand the business, the easier it becomes to say 'yes' or 'no' without the need to spend hours poring over management accounts.

Colleagues tend to appreciate leaders who make decisions decisively, and who occasionally admit when they don't have all the answers. From my experience, when I can't find a solution, it's often best to acknowledge it and seek help from the colleagues who handle the job day in and day out. They usually know precisely what to do, and they take pride in resolving the issue on my behalf. Offering them a bonus for their advice is also a great idea – after all, there's no such thing as a free lunch.

But the most critical aspect of leadership, in my view, is kindness. Kindness is not a sign of weakness. In fact, you can be both highly commercial and kind at the same time. I encourage my leaders to be kind to everyone they encounter, whether it's our customers, suppliers, or colleagues. Developing a corporate culture where kindness is the norm is essential, but it's the leaders who set the tone. Neglecting to greet everyone in the office, failing to remember names, or forgetting to send a condolence card to a colleague who has experienced a loss can quickly erode the loyalty of your team. If you love and respect your people, they'll sense it and respond in kind. Your love for your team will drive your success as a leader.

In my final message to newly promoted colleagues, I emphasize their role within the company. Despite their prestigious job titles, generous compensation, flashy cars, and luxury vacations, they are not inherently more important than anyone else in the business. The sooner they grasp this concept, the more successful they will become. By recognizing that their success hinges on the achievements and happiness of those they lead, they're more likely to be the best bosses their teams have ever had.

THE POWER OF GRATITUDE IN LEADERSHIP

Sometimes when we're at work, the phrase 'thank you' can fall by the wayside. Gratitude, however, should be a fundamental part of any successful leader's repertoire. Daily doses of praise, generous compliments, and heartfelt expressions of appreciation should sit proudly at the top of your daily to-do list. It's not just a matter of politeness; it's good business sense. Engaged and happy employees tend to perform better and exhibit greater loyalty, while the most potent antidote to workplace dissatisfaction is a hearty helping of gratitude.

Gratitude is not only a morale booster; it's the powerhouse behind happiness, friendship formation, and resilience against adversity. While it might seem like the latest trend in leadership and wellbeing, scientists have been studying its effects for years. Our capacity for gratitude is embedded in our biological makeup and forms bonds among people. In fact, even our primate relatives share food for mutual benefit, which has evolved into our capacity to be thankful for acts of kindness. This sentiment encourages us to reciprocate with kindness, and it became evolutionarily advantageous to form enduring, trusted relationships based on gratitude. This ancient concept even gave rise to the popular phrase, 'You scratch my back, and I'll scratch yours'.

The scientific evidence for the benefits of gratitude is compelling. Individuals who have experienced gratitude tend to be happier, more content with their lives, sleep better, maintain healthier relationships, and are less prone to depression, addiction, and burnout. The positive effects extend to the workplace as well. Working diligently without receiving any acknowledgement can lead to negative thoughts and diminished performance. Within an organizational culture, it's easy to identify when one has been wronged, but it's less common to celebrate success.

Though genetics, culture, and personality play vital roles, employers hold a crucial piece of the gratitude puzzle. Establishing a Gratitude Department to spot and reward anything amazing isn't enough. It's about infusing gratitude into your leadership style and culture.

Frequent bonuses may seem like the answer, but money isn't the only motivator. Plus, if you only give out a reward once a year, how do you ensure sustained motivation for the remaining 364 days in the calendar?

Count Your Pebbles

There's a story that I love about a Chief Executive who practised a simple yet profoundly impactful ritual each day. Every day, before he walked through the office and down through the factory floor, he put five small pebbles into his right pocket. The purpose of these pebbles? To act as a physical reminder to prompt him to express gratitude. Each time he recognized a team member's outstanding effort or contribution, he moved one of the pebbles from his right pocket to his left. This commitment to acknowledging and appreciating his team created a culture of gratitude within the organization.

The pebbles were not just a reminder to say thank you; they symbolized recognition and appreciation. As they moved from one pocket to the other, they signified the acknowledgement of hard work, dedication, and success. Having a company culture where everyone feels appreciated and recognized for their contributions is a sure-fire way to show each member of the team that the boss values them.

As leaders, it's our responsibility to serve as the Director of Gratitude, ensuring every opportunity to say 'Well done' is spotted, and our colleagues know how much we value their contributions. It's one of the simplest ways to earn money, gain happy customers, and foster a productive workforce.

The most effective way to express gratitude is often through the written word. A handwritten letter, sent to a colleague's home, is a personal and touching gesture that explicitly communicates appreciation. When I receive a letter or email from a customer praising the excellence of one of our colleagues, I make sure to send a handwritten letter not only to the customer but also to the colleague. The latter also receives a framed copy of the message. I make it a personal commitment to send out an average of 30 letters each week. Like the CEO who moved their pebbles from one pocket to the other, the very act of sitting down and writing out my appreciation fills me with satisfaction.

We've also established a range of symbolic gestures to convey our gratitude. These include various badges that we distribute to our colleagues, which they proudly wear on their aprons and lanyards. The badges themselves say things like: 'Community Champion': for the colleague who has made a real difference to the community, or 'Mental Health': for the colleague who acts as a mental health first aider and 'I'm a Mentor': for the colleague who is an incredible mentor to others. We adopted this idea after being inspired by a visit to Walmart's headquarters in Bentonville, Arkansas. Their museum featured a wall filled with different badges that associates had received over the years as rewards for exceptional actions. The impact of such a simple gesture should never be underestimated.

In addition to badges, our colleagues treasure a simple reward: scratch cards. We've created our own cards, with prizes ranging from small financial rewards to 'A meal out on James' (worth at least £50), a bottle of their choice, and my personal favourite, 'The next sale is yours', which gives the colleague who receives it the monetary value of their next sale. Everyone loves to be appreciated, no matter what they win.

Incorporating gratitude into your leadership approach isn't just about issuing the occasional 'thank you'. It's about cultivating a culture where acknowledging and celebrating successes is the norm.

Top 5 tips for showing gratitude:

1. **Express Appreciation:** Take the time to regularly acknowledge your team's hard work and contributions with sincerity.
2. **Handwritten Notes:** Write a personal note or letter of genuine appreciation and send it to your colleagues' homes for a more personal touch.

3. **Symbolic Gestures:** Introduce badges, pins, or other small tokens of recognition that can be worn or displayed with pride.
4. **Surprise Rewards:** Use scratch cards or other unpredictable rewards to keep the spirit of gratitude alive and exciting.
5. **Feedback Mechanism:** Encourage open dialogue and feedback within your team to make gratitude a two-way street.

A PATH TO GROWTH: MISTAKES MAKE YOU AND YOUR TEAM STRONGER

It's not uncommon to encounter narratives filled with tales of unmitigated success and picture-perfect outcomes in many business books. In these accounts, everything seems to unfold seamlessly, and triumph follows triumph. However, the reality is often far less glamorous. Not every idea comes to fruition as planned, and the journey to success can be riddled with pitfalls, setbacks, and miscalculations. This raises an important question: is it better for a business to steer clear of mistakes altogether, or should it actively embrace them as part of the process?

Mistakes should be seen as an essential part of the pursuit of perfection. They provide invaluable opportunities to gain experience, refine decision-making skills, and learn from the past. The critical factor here is not about avoiding errors at all costs but about ensuring that we don't repeat the same mistake twice, all while managing the process so that it doesn't lead to financial ruin. It's a journey where even small missteps can prove costly, while significant blunders can sometimes be disastrous.

Sir James Dyson's Story

In the field of entrepreneurship, one iconic name stands out: Sir James Dyson. Not so long ago, he revealed the extraordinary journey he took to transform his unique ideas into a successful empire. Dyson is known for his pioneering work in the realm of vacuum cleaners, but his path to success was far from a smooth one. His story, featured in his book, *Invention*, is an inspiring tale of resilience, determination, and the value of making mistakes.

In 1974, Dyson embarked on his quest to create the world's first bagless vacuum cleaner. However, it wasn't an easy journey. To perfect his revolutionary dust separator, he designed and tested a staggering 5,087 prototypes. That's right, he didn't stop at a handful of attempts, but relentlessly pursued his vision for a vacuum cleaner that could provide efficient suction without the hassle of bags. His unwavering determination and financial resilience, combined with a willingness to learn from each mistake, eventually paid off.

What this illustrates is the tremendous importance of making mistakes as part of the learning process. It's vital to view mistakes as stepping stones on the path to innovation and perfection. Dyson's willingness to push the boundaries of conventional thought and persevere through thousands of prototypes helped him create a game-changing product that disrupted the vacuum cleaner industry. It's not that mistakes were deliberately sought after; rather, they were embraced as an integral part of the journey towards perfection.

Similarly, the story of the Rocket Chemical Company, founded by three scientists in San Diego in 1953, offers a valuable lesson in determination. Their aim was to develop rust-prevention solvents and degreasers for the aerospace industry, and they encountered 39 failed attempts before finally finding a solution. Their water displacement formula still remains unchanged and is known worldwide as WD40.

The lesson from both Dyson and Rocket's stories is clear: errors and mishaps should be seen as opportunities for growth. They provide valuable insights and help us make better decisions in the future. The key is not to repeat the same mistake twice, and to ensure that the lessons learned from failures become positive forces behind future successes.

PASSION AND PERSEVERANCE: THE SECRETS TO SUCCESS

Psychologist Angela Duckworth, in her book *Grit*, reveals that success is not merely a product of genius but rather a fusion of passion and perseverance. I acknowledge that while I'm not the most skilled cobbler or key cutter, the success of Timpson is partly rooted in a combination of my enthusiasm and competitiveness. The relentless pursuit of having the best shops and the happiest colleagues on the high street has, at times, created its share of challenges and financial hiccups, but I remain committed to this vision.

It may sound counterintuitive, but I want to keep making mistakes, as through trying and failing you end up with a better business. Using the words 'sorry, I messed up' should be a more common occurrence in business.

Mistakes: the three-fold breakdown
Strategic errors
These errors are often the most costly and can have far-reaching consequences. A case in point is Timpson's decision to diversify by acquiring a manufacturer of house signs and letterboxes in 2005. While the company was well-structured and conveniently located near our office, it quickly became evident that we lacked the required expertize to manage a foundry. Shops are much easier to manage. The competitive nature of the market didn't make it any better, and we found ourselves at odds with retail giants like B&Q and Homebase. Eventually, the business had to be sold in 2010, and we were happy to get our money back. These errors, although expensive, provide valuable lessons that guide future decisions. We quickly realized that we're only good at a few specific things.

Operational mistakes
These are often more insightful than painful, as they present opportunities for learning and growth. For instance, when Timpson delved into online retailing, the experience was less than smooth. The 'City Cobbler' project, where we provided a same-day shoe repair service in London, faced several operational challenges and one big PR disaster, when Keith, our delivery man, fell off his bike while on the way to the Evening Standard office who were testing our new service. While these

mistakes may not be as financially damaging, they are rich sources of knowledge.

People mistakes
These errors revolve around individuals, and they can be the most emotionally taxing. Over-promoting a colleague is one such error, and it can lead to challenges that must be addressed. While people mistakes may not be as financially costly as strategic errors, they have a profound impact on individuals, creating emotional distress for colleagues and their families.

One of the ways that Timpson fosters a culture of learning from mistakes is by encouraging colleagues on the front lines to innovate and take calculated risks. While many companies have a plethora of rules and guidelines aimed at preventing even the smallest errors, we employ a refreshingly different approach. With just two core rules – 'put the money in the till' and 'look the part' – colleagues are allowed and encouraged to explore new ideas, bypassing conventional guidelines and sign-off processes. This approach acknowledges that those on the front lines are often the best innovators. By removing the restrictions that might stifle creativity, companies can harness the collective intelligence and problem-solving capacity of their entire team. The best ideas come from those furthest from the boardroom.

A culture of honesty and learning from failure
In a culture where honesty is prized and the celebration of failure is not only accepted but encouraged, companies can

harness the power of mistakes to develop better businesses, enhance customer satisfaction, and foster engaged and motivated colleagues. It's undeniable that every mistake carries a cost, but, in the grand scheme of progress, it's akin to a tortoise extending its neck – a necessary risk for making meaningful strides.

Perhaps in the future, there will be a business award that celebrates the most meaningful mistake. If such an accolade comes to be, Timpson is poised to be a formidable contender. The journey of learning from mistakes has been our compass, guiding us towards success, one error at a time.

EFFICIENT AND PRODUCTIVE BOARD MEETINGS

Being invited to sit on a board is an accomplishment that few individuals ever experience. Along with this privilege comes the responsibility to make critical decisions that ensure the company's survival, compliance with the law, and the welfare of its employees. Many people anticipate that board meetings, often seen from a distance as the apex of corporate life, will be well-structured and productive. However, all too often, they turn out to be tedious, disorganized, and unproductive gatherings. Participants might appear to be merely filling the seats, while genuine business decisions are hashed out informally over coffee or in pre-meeting discussions. But it doesn't have to be this way.

Board meetings should be engaging, informative, and everyone present should leave with a clear understanding of the company's main strategic goals, and their specific roles in achieving them. While the topics may sometimes be serious, that doesn't mean the atmosphere has to be sombre and overly formal. A well-prepared chair plays a pivotal role in making board meetings efficient and productive.

An exceptional chair, acting as the conductor of the meeting, can bring out the best in the board members. On the contrary, a poor chair may allow politics and ego clashes to dominate the discussion, meetings to drag on, and important decisions to get overlooked. To maintain a constructive atmosphere, every member should feel comfortable expressing their views in an environment that promotes honesty and kindness.

I recall my first Trustee Board meeting at Tate, the British art institution, where Lord John Browne, previously CEO of BP and a seasoned board member of various companies including Goldman Sachs and Intel, presided as Chair. John adeptly led the meeting, ensuring that all board members participated, that major topics were discussed productively, and that the meeting adhered to its schedule. His method of summarizing the contributions made by trustees after each topic was discussed, making immediate decisions when clear, and charting a course of action for more complex matters, was a masterclass in leadership for any type of meeting, whether it was a company board or a casual discussion among colleagues.

At Timpson, we have established some unwritten rules for our board meetings. We assume that the five of us (with my father John serving as Chair, Paresh Majithia as our FD, and myself as an executive, along with Sarah Dunning and Stephen Robertson as non-executives) are well-versed in the business and have thoroughly reviewed the board pack. We convene just six times a year, including one overnight session. We take pride in keeping the board pack concise, around one centimetre thick, which is sent out a week before the meeting. This ensures that we don't spend our time sifting through papers and late additions. We focus our discussions on two or three pivotal strategic topics. After deliberations between my father, Paresh, and myself, my father drafts a brief paper outlining the key strategic concepts for the meeting, which then becomes the meeting agenda.

Our meetings commence at 10 a.m. and consistently adjourn by 1 p.m., just in time for lunch at our Cobbler Café. Board meetings and a round of golf are best accomplished within three hours. To adhere to our schedule, we refrain from revisiting the previous meeting's minutes, which are disseminated with updates under each topic in red ink, ensuring that all unresolved issues are addressed and action plans are in place before the next meeting starts. This simple approach saves us at least 30 minutes of each meeting.

Occasionally, the auditors' presentation of the annual accounts may pose a challenge. Auditors tend to delve into great detail, and without constraints, their session can drag on for hours. To address this, we have managed to compress the audit presentation to as short as 20 minutes. We believe that the role of the board is not to scrutinize every detail but to place trust in the executive team's competence.

Board meetings are essential, but one board that typically leaves members with little satisfaction is the 'remco' board, responsible for determining the senior team's compensation and bonus arrangements. In larger public companies, consultants often sit on these boards to provide information on market trends, effectively following the crowd. We believe that effective boards should not merely follow trends but should instead focus on exploring unconventional and innovative ideas.

Effective boards recognize that while they have the authority to make decisions, they need the insight and support of the front-line employees to achieve those decisions. Sitting in an office making decisions without experiencing the shop floor and listening to colleagues' perspectives is counterproductive. These individuals are often the ones who are best equipped to understand customer needs and suggest innovative ways to improve the business. While we have a small board of five members, the primary decision-makers are those who serve customers.

It is vital to emphasize the significance of well-structured and quick meetings, effective notetaking, and adherence to the meeting's structure. In this age of remote working, where colleagues may not be physically present but participate via virtual platforms, it is paramount that meetings are conducted with clarity, succinctness, and efficiency. Minimizing the formality and maximizing the focus on the meeting's agenda ensures that every participant leaves the meeting room with a clear understanding of their roles in achieving the company's goals and strategies.

Easy wins to keep your meetings short and effective
Prepare and circulate an agenda in advance
Send out an agenda well before the meeting so participants can prepare, ensuring everyone knows the topics to be

discussed, and ban late papers. They should also be fun. The more laughter you hear in a board meeting the more engaged the team will be.

Appoint a timekeeper

Designate someone to keep an eye on the clock and gently remind participants when time for a specific topic is up, preventing lengthy discussions.

Stick to the agenda

Avoid veering off-topic and maintain a structured discussion. If unrelated issues arise, park them for a separate discussion.

Encourage concise updates

Ask participants to deliver updates in a concise manner, focusing on key points. This helps avoid long-winded reports.

Summarize and assign action items

End each meeting by summarizing key takeaways and assigning action items to specific team members, ensuring accountability and clarity.

The above tips can help streamline meetings, keep them on track, and make them more productive, but it is important to ensure that they work for your business and the team you interact with on a day-to-day basis. However, it is always better to have a minimal 'meeting culture' in order to allow your team – and you – the time to be on the front line, where the best ideas are found.

ADDRESSING THE ROOM: GETTING OVER A FEAR OF PUBLIC SPEAKING

Glassaphobia (n.) [glas-uh-foh-bee-uh]

Glassaphobia is the fear or intense anxiety associated with speaking in public or addressing an audience. It often results in physical symptoms like sweating, trembling, and difficulty in delivering speeches or presentations. Glassaphobia can range from mild nervousness to severe panic and avoidance of public speaking situations. It is a common fear and can be overcome with practice and techniques to manage anxiety.

When I was sixteen, I was asked to read a lesson out in the school chapel. I practised over and over, again and again, every day for a month, just so that I could recite it word for word with my eyes shut, never missing a beat. But when it came to the day of the recital, I could barely stand up. My legs were shaking so much out of fear that I thought I was going to fall over. This early experience with public speaking was a hard lesson, and I understand the anxiety that people feel when having to get themselves ready to address a room. Although it wasn't the best of starts, it did teach me the importance of preparation, from remembering what you're going to say to being able to have that information at the front of your mind, as if it were second nature. It is something I have carried with me throughout my time as CEO and at other times when I am talking to the people I don't work with.

Richard Greene AKA The Master of Charisma, a speech coach and adviser to presidents, princesses, and others, has been a significant influence on my public speaking journey. He advised me to become a storyteller, like Martin Luther King, remembered for his ill-fated 1968 'I've Been to the Mountaintop' speech in support of striking sanitation workers in Memphis. King's eloquence and narrative style chimed with the audience, and his message continues to reverberate to this day. So, whether you're addressing a small gathering or a vast audience, starting your speech with the words 'Let me tell you a story' can captivate your listeners' attention and set the stage for an engaging dialogue.

Greene's analysis of effective speeches underscores that content, while crucial, contributes only 7 per cent to the speech's impact, with voice tone at 38 per cent and body language at 55 per cent. The way you convey your message matters much more than the words themselves. When Richard was asked to name the best political speakers, he mentioned Bill Clinton, highlighting the power of body language, as well as Barack Obama, renowned for his calm, consistent tone. What these individuals share is a mastery of their chosen medium of communication, transcending the boundaries of spoken language.

While there are several pitfalls to avoid when delivering a speech, a strong opener can set the tone for success. The role of the compere, or introducer, is critical if you're being introduced on the stage in front of others. Briefing them beforehand ensures a smooth beginning ahead of your speech, as a badly executed introduction, such as pronouncing a name incorrectly or introducing the wrong person, can start you off on the wrong foot, and affect your connection with the audience. Your audience should be primed to follow you throughout the speech, ready to listen to what you have to say with eager ears, not looking to see if you are the right person up there!

Another valuable technique for grabbing your audience's attention is beginning with a simple token of gratitude. Lord David Ramsbotham, a former Chief Inspector of Prisons, and Army General, always begins his speeches by thanking everyone that's present, from the caterers to the sound technicians, and most importantly, the audience. His warmth and appreciation resonate with the audience. As a leader, cultivating an atmosphere of goodwill and appreciation can help set the stage for more receptive audiences.

However, even with the best preparation and intention, public speaking doesn't always go according to plan. When I was at an awards dinner a few years ago, there was an after-dinner speaker who had been a contestant on a series of *The Apprentice*, but they struggled to connect with the audience. The energy in the room – to begin with – was full of laughter and fun, champagne flowed, and the room had buzzed with enthusiasm. About five minutes into their speech, which admittedly had somewhat of a slow start, they started shouting at everyone, telling them to 'shut up and listen' because people had quickly lost interest. Understandably, this only added fuel to the fire and made the audience go off the speaker even more. This incident underscores that success in public speaking often depends on the alignment between the speaker and the audience's expectations.

Speaking in public is never easy, but when the audience plays its part and is on your side, it's more likely to be an enjoyable experience for everyone involved. By applying these lessons and techniques, your next public speaking opportunity can become a platform to convey your message with authority, resonance, and confidence.

5 tips for getting over the nerves of speaking in public:

1. Prepare ahead – Preparation is key to feeling confident when speaking in public. Get the facts right, know what you're saying, and find a moment to relax beforehand.
2. Embrace storytelling – Start with 'Let me tell you a story' to engage your audience from the outset.
3. Delivery – How you say it matters more than what you say.
4. Master the art of a strong opener – A strong beginning sets the tone for the audience.
5. Be thankful – Start with a thank you and watch people lean in.

SG World: A Case Study in the Benefits of Flexible Working

SG World, a family-run business located in Crewe, led by Managing Director Mark Haase, has embraced a new way of working that is transforming their employees' lives. The company is in the process of adopting a four-day work week and remote working options, introducing greater flexibility for their staff.

Mark Haase's journey towards this new work paradigm began during the lockdown period, when he found himself spending more quality time with his family, enjoying regular dinners together, and going on long walks with his children. This newfound work-life balance prompted Mark to explore how SG World could permanently adopt a four-day work week while ensuring that his colleagues could also benefit from the improved lifestyle he had experienced.

Inspired by the Scandinavian model, where both the public and private sectors widely embrace a four-day work week, Mark Haase saw the potential for this transition at SG World. The challenge was to find the right trigger for making the change.

Opportunity knocked during the European Championship final, held on a Sunday in July. Mark decided to offer his colleagues an additional paid day off on the Monday, allowing them to enjoy a long weekend following the event. The positive impact was palpable, as the team returned to work with renewed enthusiasm and energy.

Recognizing the potential benefits for both employees and the company, Mark made a bold move. Just five weeks later, he announced that SG World would transition to a four-day workweek, with Fridays designated as non-working days. Employees would work slightly longer days, but an hour and a half less each week than contracted. Despite this, their salaries would remain unchanged. The initiative was well-received, and customer feedback has been overwhelmingly positive.

The 'Live Better' initiative introduced by SG World not only offers employees a better work-life balance but has also attracted new talent to the company, eager to be part of this progressive approach. This technique wouldn't work in our company, as our customers expect the shops to be open seven days a week, but for some, it's a credible option.

SG World's experience demonstrates that flexible working models can enhance employee wellbeing, improve morale, and even draw in new talent, proving that, with the right approach, flexible working can significantly benefit businesses and their employees.

In our quest for optimal time management and achieving a work-life balance, there's much to be learned from other companies like SG World, but it is key to remember that every business operates differently and has other pressures that might not suit remote working.

For me, it's crucial to set the tone for your organization from the outset. Embracing a new world of work, untethered from the traditional 9-to-5 office model, is a path worth considering. Here's how you can lead by example and champion a shift towards a more balanced work-life approach.

Prioritize work-life balance
Demonstrate a commitment to work-life balance in your own life. Encourage your team to do the same by setting reasonable expectations for work hours and respecting personal time.

Embrace flexibility
In the new world of work, flexibility is paramount. Consider implementing flexible work arrangements such as occasional remote working or compressed work weeks.

Encourage personal growth
Advocate for personal growth and development, both professionally and personally. Support your team in pursuing their passions outside of work.

Value productivity over presence
Shift the focus from where and when work is done to the quality and productivity of the work itself. Trust your team to deliver results, regardless of their physical location.

Company-wide changes: finding the right balance
While leaders play a pivotal role, achieving a work-life balance often necessitates broader organizational changes. It's essential to strike a balance between business operations and individual wellbeing. Here's how to align your company's goals with a more harmonious work environment:

A hybrid model of work
Embrace a hybrid model where employees can choose between working at the office or remotely. This can empower your team to tailor their work environment to their specific needs.

The power of four-day work weeks
Consider the example of SG World, which successfully transitioned to a four-day work week. While this change might not suit every industry, it offers enhanced work-life balance, and can be an attractive proposition for both current and potential employees.

Making time for what matters
Encourage your colleagues to prioritize what matters most to them outside of work. Whether it's spending time with family, pursuing hobbies, or taking up new interests, a harmonious life complements a productive work life.

Flexibility as a perk
Recognize flexibility as a valuable perk in the modern workforce. It can be a powerful tool for attracting and retaining top talent.

Positive outcomes and a happier workforce

The key takeaway is that work should now focus on the outcomes, not the hours spent doing it. In leading by example and implementing organizational changes that value a healthy work-life balance, you can create a more positive, productive, and content workforce. This approach not only benefits your team's wellbeing but also enhances the success and longevity of your business.

The future of work is rapidly changing and, as we have discussed, to thrive in this new world, businesses and leaders must be open to innovative work arrangements and prioritize the wellbeing of their employees. Forward-thinking companies underscore the value of embracing flexibility, a more balanced work week and personal fulfilment as essential elements of the modern workplace.

What Have We Learned?

Kindness starts at the top

Leadership plays a pivotal role in fostering kindness and empathy within an organization. Leaders should set the tone for company culture by exemplifying kindness, and demonstrating that it's not a sign of weakness. Creating a culture of kindness begins with leaders who prioritize the wellbeing and happiness of both employees and customers.

Adapting to new work patterns

In today's world, flexibility and adaptability are paramount. Leaders could embrace new work patterns to support their teams and enhance overall efficiency. Recognizing that the traditional 9-to-5 model is not the only path to success allows leaders to accommodate evolving employee needs.

Clear and concise language

Effective communication relies on clear and concise language. Leaders must avoid jargon and ensure that their messages are easily understood by all team members. Simplifying communication fosters better understanding, alignment, and a more productive work environment. Providing straightforward explanations and instructions enables colleagues to make informed decisions and act with confidence. It's ok to say no.

Give support when actioning promotions

The promotion of colleagues into leadership roles is a critical process requiring care and support. Leaders should offer guidance and advice to those starting their leadership journeys, to help them excel from the start. Recognizing the importance of nurturing newly promoted executives ensures a smoother transition and a higher chance of success for both individuals and the company.

Be consistent with meetings

Meetings are an essential part of business operations and should be structured and run efficiently. Leaders should aim for fewer and shorter, more focused meetings that respect participants' time and maintain their engagement. Consistency in meeting structure and following up on previous discussions, actions, and minutes helps ensure clarity, accountability, and progress within the organization.

LESSON SEVEN

NAVIGATING DIFFICULT SITUATIONS IN THE WORKPLACE

Every company comes with its own unique set of trials and tribulations. In **Lesson Seven**, we will explore the intricate art of handling difficult challenges in the workplace. As we progress through this lesson, we will build on the nuances of managing acquisitions (previously covered in (**Lesson Five** on page 143), looking to the wisdom of our mistakes, and extending a helping hand to colleagues facing personal hardships.

Every business leader should understand the need for adapting their strategies and styles, and accepting that there are usually others who are much better than them and have already found the right answers.

Throughout this lesson, we'll explore the allure of diversifying and taking on new challenges, including the positive and negative impacts, and we will look to demystify the belief that if someone can run a single business successfully, they can master any industry. The truth? They can't. We'll look at success stories, like Disney's seamless expansion into theme parks and cruise ships, and other cautionary tales, such as HMV's costly foray into live events. These examples will show the importance of recognizing the diverse skill sets that are required for different industries.

The journey of entrepreneurship is paved with mistakes, and it's through these missteps that we often learn our greatest lessons. We will uncover the truth behind why new ventures frequently take far longer to succeed than you expect, and how the pain of financial setbacks can impact the whole company. The case of our Max Spielmann photo business serves as a poignant example, showcasing the determination required to weather the storms of a new endeavour. This lesson will emphasize the value of resilience, and the ability to learn from failures as an integral part of your success.

Challenges aren't limited to while we are at work. Colleagues often face personal hardships away from the intensity of the shop floor that require understanding and support. We will discuss the benefits of extending a helping hand to those dealing with health issues, financial insecurity, and family matters.

Furthermore, we will unravel the intricate web of rules and processes that often dominate organizations, causing them to focus too much on the made-up rules which can restrict opportunities and make the office feel more like a school than a place where adults work in collaboration and with trust. More rules rarely equate to more control, or financial success. We will challenge the conventional wisdom that more rules equate to better control, and advocate for a culture where trust reigns supreme. Instead, clarity and autonomy are the driving forces behind innovation within a company, but it takes a great team behind you, who exemplify and live by the company culture, to see that fewer rules leads to greater results.

Now, let's dig in to those difficult situations at work and understand how best to navigate them.

Rule-breakers often make the best colleagues.

LESSON SEVEN

ENTREPRENEURITIS

This 'condition' may not be found in medical journals, but it's a term I've coined to describe the often-misguided notion held by some entrepreneurs that they can successfully venture into any business and make it thrive. Entrepreneuritis has, at times, afflicted my own career as we sought to diversify our business in response to the various challenges we encountered along the way. The journey hasn't been smooth sailing, and more often than not, we found ourselves navigating uncharted waters, and learned that we're only good at a few specific areas of the business world.

Most entrepreneurs can recount the rollercoaster-like journeys they've undertaken. These journeys are characterized by copious amounts of hard work, a few fortunate breaks, and, more often than not, running out of money – sometimes more than once. Despite these challenges, entrepreneurs often reach a point where they have both the capital and the enthusiasm to tackle new industries, believing that if they can successfully run one business, they can run any business.

Diversification can indeed bolster some businesses, making them more resilient and successful. Having multiple profit streams can be advantageous. The more legs a table has, the more stable it is. For instance, Disney expanded its operations from cartoons to theme parks and, more recently, cruise ships, evolving into a conglomerate worth over $300 billion. However, diversification doesn't always pan out as planned.

Take the example of HMV, a once-prominent music retailer that was a fixture on many high streets. In 2009, HMV diversified by acquiring the live events business Mama for £46 million.

Three years later, they were forced to sell it for a mere £9 million. Owning music retail shops didn't translate into the ability to sell live music event tickets. The live events industry required entirely different skills and expertize.

At Timpson, we also ventured into diversification. The core business of shoe repairs saw declining sales trends dating back to the 1960s, prompting us to seek alternative revenue streams. Over the past two decades, we acquired 16 companies, each time believing that we could apply the same techniques and cultural principles that had fuelled our core business. This strategy proved successful when we acquired other shoe repair chains, however, when we ventured beyond our comfort zone, we faced a rude awakening.

One notable case was our acquisition of Max Spielmann, a once-thriving chain of photo processing shops based in Cheshire with locations across the UK. The rise of digital photography and mobile phones had ushered in the digital revolution, leading to a decline in the analogue photography market. Entrepreneuritis struck us when we saw Max Spielmann fall into administration in 2008. We acquired the business and introduced our style of management.

It didn't take long for us to realize that we were out of our depth in the world of photography. The photo labs were expensive to maintain and often broke down. We inherited a vast warehouse filled with frames and photo paper, items we had little knowledge of. Furthermore, the majority of Max Spielmann's colleagues were female, while Timpson was predominantly a male-dominated business. We faced a steep learning curve.

Starting new ventures typically involves at least three years of trial and error, setbacks, financial investment, and, at times tears, before a business begins to show promise. In the case of Max Spielmann, it took us five years to reach a point where we could consider it a viable business with a culture as strong as at Timpson. If it hadn't been for the support of our robust Timpson business, we might have faltered.

Fortunately, we inherited dedicated and exceptional colleagues at Max Spielmann, who embraced our culture of trust and kindness. We also encountered a stroke of luck. Many other players in the photo industry gave up, allowing us to emerge as a major player. We expanded further by acquiring photo shops that had gone bankrupt and purchasing various photo chains, including Snappy Snaps. Today, our photo division generates a turnover of £100 million. However, not all our diversification attempts have been as successful.

One of the most peculiar diversification journeys, often undertaken by entrepreneurs, involves buying a local pub. In my case, my parents owned a holiday home in Anglesey, and my late mother, Alex, loathed cooking. The local pub, The White Eagle, was a neglected establishment with terrible food but was in a great location, and it was on the verge of going under. Without conducting any financial appraisals, or possessing any catering experience, my parents bought the pub. Their vision was to transform it into a thriving family holiday gastro pub, also meaning my mum didn't have to cook. This was a classic case of entrepreneuritis.

Since then, business at The White Eagle has been booming. We even went on to open another hospitality venture nearby, The Oyster Catcher, and a ski hotel in Morzine, Le Tremplin. Today, these are thriving businesses. Nevertheless, it took a gruelling ten-year journey filled with numerous near white flag moments. Each time I visit Anglesey, I am reminded that the skills required to succeed as a publican are not within my skill set. Consequently, my wife, Roisin, who is better suited to the hospitality industry, oversees the business. She relies on a remarkable team of experts to handle operations. We simply transfer the best aspects of the Timpson culture to aid our colleagues in delivering exceptional service.

Recognizing your limitations

Reflecting on my tenure as CEO two decades ago, it is crucial to acknowledge the positive and negative aspects of venturing into new business realms. The phenomenon of entrepreneuritis, where we believe that the success of one business venture guarantees triumph in others, is a double-edged sword.

The allure of entering new markets with high hopes is often paired with the harsh reality that such ventures can falter. The road to establishing a new business can be fraught with obstacles, requiring time, effort, and financial resources. A minimum of three years of mistakes, setbacks, and financial investments are often necessary before a new venture starts to show promise. By the fifth year you should have worked it out, if you can afford to wait that long.

But how do you determine if your new business venture is worth the investment of your time, effort, and capital? Here are some hints and tips, along with questions to ask yourself, to evaluate whether a new business aligns with your organization's values and objectives.

Is It Worth It?

Will it benefit the company?

Consider whether the new venture complements your existing business and helps it grow. Does it create synergies or enhance your current offerings?

At Timpson, our decisions to diversify into related businesses like watch repairs and key cutting were based on the notion that these services would complement our existing portfolio. Given the lessons we've learned from our ventures into the hospitality industry, if it doesn't align with our business aims, we don't take it on.

Will the new company fit into our culture?

Assess whether the new venture can seamlessly integrate into your organization's culture, values, and principles.

When looking to acquire other businesses, we prioritize companies whose culture aligns with our ethos of a happy, colleague-centric business that puts team members front and centre.

Is it going to be more work than it's worth?

Analyse whether the additional workload, resources, and responsibilities required for the new venture outweigh the potential benefits.

While we've ventured into various new businesses at Timpson, we have recognized that some diversification efforts are more demanding than others. We've learned to prioritize and allocate resources efficiently to ensure that the new venture is worth the investment.

FEWER RULES, GREATER OPPORTUNITY

In recent years, businesses have had to evolve and adapt to changing working patterns, which has seen a noticeable shift in the way leaders approach rules and processes. The layers of rules and regulations that have accumulated over the years often hinder, rather than facilitate, success. More rules do not equate to better outcomes; in fact, they can stifle innovation, and impose unnecessary costs and unwanted delays.

With people's shifting working patterns, companies have an opportunity to rethink their approach to rules and guidelines. The remote work environment has demonstrated that great people don't require an abundance of rules. Instead, they thrive when given the freedom and trust to showcase their creative potential.

One example that illustrates the counterproductive nature of excessive rules involves a leading FTSE 100 company's mandate that employees must always hold the handrail when using a staircase, and not walk and use their phone at the same time. I've even heard of rules that dictate when people can go to the toilet, or use their phone to speak to a loved one in distress. Who makes up these rules?

In the 1960s, the Timpson shoe repair business adhered to a military-style approach, characterized by standing orders, operating procedures, checklists, and unannounced inspections. Despite this there were still opportunities for ingenuity within the rules, even in an environment where you were expected to adhere to very specific and stringent policies.

However, what sets us apart today is our enthusiasm for allowing colleagues freedom to innovate and challenge established rules. We discovered that colleagues who occasionally bent the rules were often the ones driving the most significant improvements. Rule-breakers became some of our best colleagues, enhancing sales, customer service, and profitability. It's easier to take the rules away and let people innovate in a culture of freedom and trust. But, the reason we ventured into watch repairs was because we encourage rule breaking. It all started with Glenn Edwards, a trained watch repairer who joined us with an aspiration to explore cobbling. To boost sales, he took it upon himself to repair watches on the side, recording the transactions under the engraving button on the till. As someone who was new to our culture, Glenn anticipated that he would be reprimanded for his initiative if caught. Instead, we observed that his sales increased by 20 per cent, and we recognized it as a brilliant idea. Today, we stand as the UK's largest watch repairer, all thanks to Glenn's innovation. Breaking unnecessary rules is often very profitable.

As I've shared before, our company abides by just two straightforward rules. First, put the money in the till – in essence, ensure that financial transactions are properly recorded. The second rule is about standards – our colleagues must look the part. Colleagues are expected to behave in a manner that would make their grandparents proud. Shops need to open on time, colleagues should maintain a smart appearance, wear a tie and a badge, and they should refrain from smoking or eating in the shop. Beyond these two fundamental rules, we encourage our colleagues to exercise their judgment and apply their creativity.

We entrust our colleagues with the authority to order the stock they want, take breaks as they see fit, design store displays according to their preferences, repaint the shop if they believe it will enhance the customer experience, offer discounts, and negotiate deals. In fact, approximately 4 per cent of all our transactions are done for free. This practice, which may appear counterintuitive, has proven to be one of the most profitable aspects of our business. Customers invariably remember acts of kindness and rule-breaking, and when executed judiciously, can earn admiration and of course repeat business. The more jobs we do for free, the more money we seem to make.

DEALING WITH DISHONESTY IN THE WORKPLACE

In leadership, managing a team and ensuring its integrity and honesty can be a challenging but entirely necessary task. As CEO, I've often faced situations that require having difficult conversations with dishonest colleagues. It's a lesson I've learned the hard way, and it's a challenge that many businesses must confront, but prefer to avoid.

Confronting dishonesty in the workplace is never easy, yet it's a responsibility that falls on every senior member of the team's shoulders. Some colleagues regard fiddling with their expenses as a 'perk' of the job, but for a few, it's a grave mistake that can lead to severe consequences. While we expect each colleague to uphold our core values of trust and integrity, there are those individuals who choose a different path, becoming the proverbial bad apples who consistently siphon small amounts of money for themselves under the guise of legitimate expenses. These actions may seem insignificant, but they can rapidly escalate into a significant business problem that is both costly and incredibly time-consuming.

Globally, it's estimated that approximately 5 per cent of a company's revenue is lost to fraud, with expense fiddles accounting for a significant portion of that loss. In the United States, where they even have an Association of Certified Expense Examiners, smaller businesses face an even higher percentage of loss, estimated to be 21 per cent. No matter how you look at it, the financial impact of false expense claims – and dishonesty – is a substantial driver of profit loss.

People offer various justifications for their actions. They convince themselves that 'everyone else does it', or they argue that they are 'unpaid for some of their work'. Some even believe it's 'only fair' to claim expenses for fuel used when working further from home. However, these justifications, no matter how convincing, do not change the fundamental truth: theft is theft. Often, this behaviour is rooted in greed, which is further exacerbated by the belief that they can get away with it. Unfortunately, all too often, they do. There are countless ways to manipulate financial records in the workplace, but they are all wrong and should never be tolerated. What's important is how we go about navigating this situation. Below, you will find a few things that we, at Timpson, do to discourage any untruths.

Have transparent policies from day one

Maintaining a workplace that discourages dishonesty while offering support to those facing challenges is essential. To achieve this, creating straightforward, fair, and transparent guidelines is crucial. At our company, we take pride in our straightforward guidelines. For example, we do not pay for first-class travel, whether it's for our directors, or an adviser working on specific projects. While this may have led to a change for some who were accustomed to first-class travel in other roles at different companies, it's an integral part of keeping our expense policies straightforward and aligned with our values. Consider, too, how we manage perks. In simple terms they are the same for everyone. Gone are the days when directors had the best parking spaces by the front door, and their own VIP dining room, far away from the warehouse canteen. Everyone, no matter what their seniority or pay level, should be treated the same.

The challenge of maintaining this simplicity is that the world is constantly evolving. To stay ahead of the curve, we continuously review and update our policies. Once electric cars became more common, we introduced a new addition to our policy to address the charging of electric vehicles for work purposes, including who pays for home charging and what happens when a team member stays at a friend's house. By keeping our policies up-to-date, we ensure that our team can navigate expense claims with clarity.

Supporting those who struggle

It's important to acknowledge that sometimes, team members who resort to dishonesty may be facing underlying challenges. Instead of immediately taking punitive measures, we aim to address the root causes of their actions and provide support where needed.

Here are some ways we approach this issue:

Open dialogue

Encourage open and honest conversations. Sometimes, team members may be dealing with personal or financial difficulties. It's essential to create an environment where they feel comfortable discussing their challenges without fear of retribution. If we can help them in the short term, we can retain a talented colleague who has had a wobble. People can deserve a second chance.

Mentoring and coaching

Provide access to mentors or coaches who can offer guidance and support. These experienced colleagues can help address specific issues, and guide team members toward better decision-making.

Employee Assistance Programs

Timpson has Employee Assistance Programs in place that offer counselling, financial advice, and support for various personal and work-related issues. Making these resources readily available can be a lifeline for team members facing challenges, especially when they don't want to deal directly with their manager.

Financial education

Consider offering financial education and budgeting workshops for team members. Sometimes, financial struggles can lead to desperate measures. Equipping them with the tools to manage their finances can help prevent such situations.

Recognition and reward

Acknowledge and reward team members who consistently act with honesty and integrity. Recognizing their positive behaviour not only incentivises others but also fosters a culture of trust and ethical conduct.

Navigating dishonesty within a team is a complex and delicate task, but it's essential to approach it with clarity and a focus on support. By addressing the issue at its core and offering assistance to those who need it, we can create a work environment that values integrity, and empowers every team member to make ethical choices.

Confronting dishonesty is uncomfortable for anybody. But, in tackling the issue with transparency and a commitment to creating a culture of honesty, we not only prevent dishonesty but also strengthen the integrity of our team and our company as a whole. In the end, leading with clarity and a dedication to ethical behaviour is an invaluable asset for any leader.

NAVIGATING DIFFICULT CONVERSATIONS

Aspect of Conversation	Good Conversation	Bad Conversation
• Setting the Tone	• Start with a positive tone • Be open, empathetic and kind • Acknowledge the issue calmly	• Begin negatively or aggressively • Use a confrontational tone • Blame or criticize immediately
• Listening	• Listen actively without interruption • Show empathy and understanding • Allow the other person to express themselves	• Interrupt or dominate the conversation • Dismiss or ignore the other person's perspective • Be impatient or judgmental
• Communication	• Use 'I' statements to express feelings and thoughts • Be specific about the issue	• Use 'you' statements that can sound accusatory • Speak vaguely about the problem
• Problem Solving	• Focus on finding a solution • Brainstorm together • Seek common ground	• Dwell on the problem without seeking solutions • Be inflexible and dismissive of ideas • Create a hostile or competitive atmosphere
• Emotional Regulation	• Stay calm and composed • Manage your emotions effectively • Take breaks if necessary	• Get defensive or emotional • React impulsively • Let anger or frustration dominate the conversation

• Body Language	• Maintain open and approachable body language • Make eye contact • Avoid crossing your arms	• Display defensive or closed-off body language • Avoid eye contact or stare aggressively • Cross your arms or appear confrontational
• Empathy	• Show understanding of the other person's feelings and perspective • Use phrases like, 'I understand how you feel'.	• Lack empathy or dismiss the other person's emotions • Say things like, 'You're overreacting'.
• Resolution	• Aim for a mutually beneficial resolution • Be willing to compromise • End with a clear plan of action	• Refuse to compromise or find common ground • Leave the conversation without a resolution • Escalate the conflict further

By following the guidance outlined above, you will be better equipped to structure difficult conversations that focus on clear communication. This will allow you to better recognize the reasons behind a situation, while working towards productive resolutions that benefit everyone involved.

What happens if it goes wrong and communication breaks down?

As we've already established, people problems are an inevitable part of the journey for any company. Whether it's a breakdown in communication, dishonesty, or difficult-to-navigate situations, these issues affect almost every single business at some point or another. What's important is how organizations address and navigate those particular challenges, especially when they escalate to the legal realm of employment tribunals.

Employment tribunals, while not something businesses hope to encounter, are a reality that often arises from disputes between employers and employees. These disputes can encompass a wide range of issues, from unfair dismissal and discrimination to wage disputes and breach of employment contracts. Understanding how to navigate these legal complexities is crucial for businesses of all sizes. I've seen more leaders worry about employment tribunals than how much cash they have in the bank to pay the bills.

First and foremost, employment tribunals are a good thing to get your head around because they can become a significant drain on a company's resources, both in terms of time and money. The process can be lengthy and emotional, requiring businesses to allocate valuable time and financial resources that would be better spent on other aspects of their operations.

The cost of legal representation always seems to be more than you expect it should be. Legal fees can quickly add up, making it essential for companies to assess the potential costs and benefits of pursuing, or defending, against a tribunal claim. There is an emotional cost that should be added into the mix as well.

On top of this, negative employment tribunal outcomes can result in financial penalties for businesses found to be in breach of employment laws. These penalties can vary significantly depending on the nature of the claim and the severity of the violation. Therefore, understanding the intricacies of employment law is crucial to avoid potentially costly mistakes. In some cases they have led to some businesses going under.

Trials and Tribulations

While no business hopes to find itself in an employment tribunal, being prepared and knowing how to navigate this complex legal process is essential.

Listed below, you will find the most common causes for tribunal cases as well as the best ways to be help your company avoid the situation in the first place.

Common reasons

Unfair dismissal

An employee claiming unfair dismissal can lead to an employment tribunal if they believe their termination was unjust, or did not follow proper procedures. It's crucial for companies to have clear dismissal policies and documentation in place.

Discrimination

Claims of discrimination based on factors such as race, gender, age, disability, or religion can result in an employment tribunal. Companies must ensure that their policies and practices promote fairness and equality in the workplace, and everyone in a leadership role understands their responsibilities as an employer.

Wage disputes

Issues related to wages, including unpaid salaries, overtime, or bonuses, can lead to employment tribunal claims. Maintaining accurate payroll records is essential and a legal requirement.

Breach of employment contract

The breach of an employment contract, such as failing to provide contractual benefits, can trigger an employment tribunal. Companies should ensure their employment contracts are clear, up-to-date, and legally compliant.

Harassment and bullying

Claims related to harassment, bullying, or a hostile work environment can escalate to an employment tribunal. A strong anti-harassment policy and complaint procedure is essential.

    While no business hopes to find itself in an employment tribunal, being prepared and knowing how to navigate this complex legal process is essential.

How to Avoid Tribunals

Prevention through clear policies

The first line of defence against employment tribunal claims is to prevent them from happening in the first place. Clear, comprehensive, and legally compliant HR policies and procedures can help prevent workplace disputes.

Mediation and resolution

Before a dispute escalates to an employment tribunal, consider alternative dispute resolution methods, such as mediation or arbitration. These approaches can help resolve issues more amicably and cost-effectively.

Legal consultation

If a tribunal is inevitable, seek legal counsel from experienced employment lawyers who can provide guidance on the legal process, build a strong defense, or represent your interests in a claim.

Documentation

Maintain thorough documentation of all employment-related matters, including contracts, policies, communication, and performance evaluations. Well-documented records, and clear procedures that are correctly followed can be crucial in defending against claims.

Training

Regularly train your team, especially managers and HR personnel, in employment law, discrimination prevention, and proper dismissal procedures, to reduce the risk of errors. We find the best way to train colleagues in this technical area is to regularly attend employment tribunals to watch how other companies handle themselves. This eye-opening experience reinforces the responsibility an employer has in following the law.

Settlement agreements

In many cases, it may be beneficial for both parties to reach a settlement agreement rather than proceeding to a tribunal. Such agreements can save time and money while avoiding the uncertainty of tribunal outcomes.

Employment tribunals, while often viewed as legal battles, also present an opportunity for companies to learn and grow. Rather than seeing them as solely negative experiences, businesses can use the feedback and insights gained from tribunal cases to enhance their in-house practices.

Understanding the root causes of disputes that led to the tribunal can help companies address underlying issues. For example, if a tribunal case highlights concerns about unfair dismissal procedures, a business can review and improve its termination policies.

Additionally, companies can use tribunal experiences to reinforce their commitment to fair and ethical employment practices. It's a chance to communicate to employees, customers, and stakeholders that the organization takes its responsibilities seriously and is dedicated to continuous improvement.

While employment tribunals can be daunting and expensive, they are, unfortunately, a reality that many businesses are bound to face. The key to success in navigating these legal complexities is a combination of prevention, proactive measures, legal consultation, and a willingness to learn from the experience itself. By understanding common issues leading to tribunals, having sound policies in place, and using the process as an opportunity for improvement, businesses can better manage and, in some cases, avoid the challenges of employment tribunals.

What Have We Learned?

Don't get a case of entrepreneuritis

Entrepreneurs often believe they can succeed in any business, but diversification doesn't always pan out as planned. It's crucial to recognize your limitations and focus on areas where you have expertize.

Rules and regulations

Overbearing rules can hinder innovation and success in the workplace. Companies should rethink their approach to rules, and provide employees with more freedom, creativity, and trust to showcase their creative potential.

Difficult conversations

Effective communication in difficult conversations involves setting a positive tone, active listening, clear communication, problem-solving, emotional regulation, empathy, and finding mutually beneficial resolutions.

Understand the rules

Employment tribunals can be costly and time-consuming. It's essential for businesses to have clear policies, seek legal counsel, maintain documentation, provide training, and consider alternative dispute resolution methods to prevent and manage tribunal situations effectively.

Difficult situations (like mistakes) are valuable learning tools
Instead of viewing tribunals solely as negative experiences,
businesses can use them as opportunities for improvement.
Understanding the root causes of disputes can lead to better
practices, reinforce commitment to ethics, and enhance the
organization's reputation.

LESSON EIGHT

GIVE BACK TO GET MORE

Welcome to **Lesson Eight**, where I'm excited to share some valuable insights and experiences with you. In the everyday world of business, management, and leadership, we often hear about the pursuit of profit and the relentless drive for success. These pursuits are important, but in this lesson, we'll take a different perspective.

At Timpson, we've always believed that there's more to business than just making money. We've found that when you make a commitment to give back, something remarkable happens. It's our secret formula for success that we're eager to share with you.

So, let's dive in and explore the importance of taking a traditional model and flipping it upside down. We'll discuss the profound impact of hiring ex-offenders and individuals whom society has often cast aside. You'll see that for us, it's not about a person's past mistakes but about the potential they hold for a brighter future.

We'll also delve into what it truly means to be philanthropic. You'll discover that it's not just about selfless acts but a two-way street where both companies and communities benefit. We'll unravel the stories behind our own philanthropic journey and illustrate that success in business isn't just measured in monetary gain, but by the profound impact that a company can have on society.

As we venture further, we'll explore how we provide crucial support to care leavers and ex-offenders during their early career development. You'll see the immense value of this support and the positive impact it can have on care leavers' lives and the broader community.

Additionally, we'll share the insights and lessons we've gained from this journey. You'll learn how your company can embrace the spirit of giving back to the community, discovering tips and hints for businesses keen to start their philanthropic journey. We'll guide you through the careful steps we've implemented to ensure that ex-offenders are given a fighting chance to reintegrate into society.

While this might seem to go against the 'traditional' business model of the pursuit of profit over everything else, we've learned that by giving back, you end up with more. So get started and see what benefits a culture of philanthropy can bring for your company.

TAKING THE TRADITIONAL MODEL AND FLIPPING IT UPSIDE DOWN

I have a confession to make – I don't believe in an ivory tower approach to business. My family's legacy at Timpson isn't just about offering exceptional service or mastering the art of cobbling and key cutting; it's about giving back, and doing our part to create a more inclusive and compassionate society.

Over the years, Timpson has been on an incredible journey – a journey that reflects our unwavering commitment to the wider communities that we serve with such passion. One of the most remarkable stops on this journey has been our dedication to employing ex-offenders. It's a decision that didn't come without its challenges, but it's one I wouldn't change for the world. Hiring individuals with a criminal record and providing them with a second chance has become a cornerstone of our business, and it's a commitment I'm immensely proud of.

Why do we do it? It's simple, really. Our approach isn't based solely on philanthropy or idealism; it's firmly rooted in pragmatism. When you give someone a second chance, when you trust them with a job, you're making a bet on their future. And, more often than not, that bet pays off in spades. This, again, feeds into everything we aim to achieve here at the company, from building that high-performing Super Team and trusting our colleagues to do the job as best they can, while accepting mistakes are bound to happen.

We've witnessed countless stories of transformation. Individuals who have served their time, who have learned from their mistakes, and who are eager to reintegrate into society.

They are not defined solely by their past actions; they are defined by their potential and their capacity to change. By providing employment opportunities to ex-offenders, we're helping them rebuild their lives, supporting their families, and giving them a chance to become valued, responsible members of our communities. This isn't just an altruistic act; it's a win-win for everyone involved.

Now, you might be wondering, how do we select the right candidates from this unusual pool? Our approach is quite unique, and it builds on our unique perspective on recruitment. As with all other candidates interviewing for prospective roles at Timpson, or any of our other companies, we don't care about your qualifications so why would we care about your past? We don't just look at a person's criminal record; we look beyond it. We understand that every individual has a unique story, a set of skills, and a capacity for growth. It's our job to provide them with the platform to showcase their potential. This is where the magic happens, where we give them a chance to write a new chapter. Of course, there are some people who we can't hire, to ensure the safety of our colleagues and customers, but generally speaking, if we can find the right role for that person, we will be able to make it happen for them.

Ex-offenders who join our team undergo a comprehensive training program, ensuring they have the skills they need to succeed in their roles. And, most importantly, they have the support of our incredible colleagues. In fostering an environment of acceptance and understanding here at the company, everyone gets a fair shot at being successful.

Our commitment to giving back doesn't end with our hiring practices. We've taken our dedication to criminal justice reform to a whole new level. I have the privilege of serving as the Chair of the Prison Reform Trust, a role I've held since early 2016. This charitable organization, which receives all the fees I earn for writing this book, works tirelessly to reform the prison system, and improve the lives of prisoners and their families. It is a cause that is dear to my heart, and I am genuinely committed to bringing about meaningful change. This position allows me to dive deep into the world of prisons, working first-hand with inmates, and understanding the conditions they face. It's an eye-opening experience that has only solidified my belief in the importance of second chances.

Prisons should be places of rehabilitation, not just punishment. By participating in programs and initiatives aimed at reforming our justice system, I've gained insight into the challenges and obstacles faced by those in custody. Many of them share stories of despair, longing for a chance to re-enter society as contributing members. It's a longing I can relate to on a deeply personal level, from when my mother used to take us on visits to HMP Styal when I was growing up because she was a foster parent and often looked after the children of these prisoners.

In addition to my work with the Prison Reform Trust, we've established the Timpson Foundation, an entity dedicated to creating opportunities and empowering individuals to lead better lives. The foundation supports various initiatives, from providing holidays and experiences for foster families, to offering financial assistance to disadvantaged families. It's our way of extending our reach beyond the workplace and our immediate team, permitting us to touch and better the lives of those who need it most.

The lesson is clear: it pays to give back to the community. Our commitment to employing ex-offenders, my role at the

Prison Reform Trust, and the wider endeavours of the Timpson Foundation all reflect our unwavering belief in the transform-ative power of second chances, and the importance of community involvement. Success isn't solely measured in prof-its; it's measured in the positive impact we make, the lives we change, and the opportunities we provide. By embracing an ethos of giving back, we, as both businesses and individuals, can pave the way for a brighter and more compassionate future.

One of the most heartening aspects of our work has been witnessing the transformative power of second chances. Our commitment to hiring ex-offenders isn't merely a matter of providing employment; it's about enabling individuals to regain their dignity and rebuild their lives. The statistics speak for themselves, with studies showing that ex-offenders who find employment are far less likely to reoffend. In essence, this approach serves as a pathway to break the cycle of reoffending and, in turn, leads to safer communities.

My role at the Prison Reform Trust has provided me with a unique and invaluable perspective on the criminal justice system in the UK. It's a responsibility I wholeheartedly embrace, as it allows me to advocate for much-needed change in a prison system not fit for purpose.

The first and perhaps most crucial aspect of my role is bridging the gap between the general public and those in pris-ons. It's all too easy for society to distance itself from the lives and struggles of those behind bars. My involvement with the prisons enables me to keep these individuals firmly in the public eye, ensuring that their needs and concerns are heard and, on some occasions, even meet and hire soon-to-be released people. I think the business community is now coming round to the fact that if it's good for us, it's probably good for them too.

One of the fundamental challenges we face is the perception of prisons as places of punishment rather than rehabilitation. In truth, there is a severe lack of rehabilitative measures within the prison system, making it difficult for inmates to reintegrate into society, which means a vicious cycle of release, reoffend, reincarcerate.

In my role I've been able to advocate for prison reform, pushing for a shift in focus from mere punishment to genuine rehabilitation. My interactions with prisoners have provided insight into the many barriers they face in rebuilding their lives upon release, and this knowledge fuels my passion for change.

Another significant focus of the Trust is the care and support provided to individuals dealing with mental health issues while in prison. Mental health concerns affect inmates profoundly, and yet, access to adequate care and support can be limited within the system. This lack of attention can exacerbate existing mental health issues, and lead to a higher likelihood of reoffending.

We're striving to bring about a change in this aspect, advocating for better mental health support. By ensuring that inmates receive the care and assistance they need, we're not only addressing a critical issue but also taking a crucial step towards reducing the chances of reoffending upon release.

Moreover, the support system for individuals leaving prison is equally significant. Entering society after a period of incarceration is a daunting prospect that carries its own challenges, but with the correct care and support systems in place there is the opportunity to give those people the support that they need. The stigma associated with a criminal record can severely limit job prospects, and the process of reintegration can be overwhelming. However, it's in this period that the significance of second chances becomes even more apparent.

I strongly believe that employment is a critical component of successful reintegration. It provides individuals with a sense of purpose, financial stability, and the opportunity to rebuild their lives. To support this cause, we've been working closely with various organizations to create more opportunities for ex-offenders in the workplace.

These initiatives represent just one aspect of our ongoing efforts to give back to the wider community, as we also participate in the Restart Scheme, a scheme separate to our business but one that embodies our own company culture of giving second chances and employment opportunities to individuals who face significant obstacles in their career paths. Restart is more than a scheme; it's a lifeline to those who need it most. By partnering with this program, we reaffirm our belief that everyone deserves the opportunity to rebuild their lives and secure a brighter future. The heart of our ethos is rooted in the belief that businesses have a crucial role to play in improving society. It's not merely about financial transactions; it's about creating positive change. Success, truly, should be measured by the lives we touch and the hope we bring, not just the money we make.

Hiring Ex-Offenders is a Great Thing

During a visit to HMP Thorn Cross in 2003, I was shown around the prison by an amazing tour guide called Matt. He told me that after completing his A Levels, he went out to celebrate one night and got into a fight, subsequently receiving a three-year sentence that meant he couldn't go to university.

I was so impressed by him, his personality was just what we look for. So I handed him my business card and offered him a contract of employment as soon as he was released.

A lot of people – business leaders included – might think it's strange to recruit people from prison, and trust them to serve the public, but it makes good business sense to me. Every company wants great people, but it's not always easy to find the best using traditional hiring techniques.

Matt is still with us, as are over 600 other ex-offenders we have taken on, making up over 10 per cent of our workforce. It may sound strange that a key cutting business employs reformed burglars and drug dealers, but customers understand that they want great service from great people, and are happy to support a company giving disadvantaged people a second chance.

Success isn't solely measured in profits; it's measured in the positive impact we make, the lives we change, and the opportunities we provide.

WHAT DOES IT MEAN TO BE PHILANTHROPIC?

The power of philanthropy and corporate social responsibility is never more evident than in the stories of remarkable individuals and businesses that choose to give back to the community. We are reminded of the incredible spirit of generosity exemplified by Captain Tom, whose inspiring journey of walking 100 laps of his garden – one for each year of this legendary centenarian's life – during the UK lockdowns raised over £38 million for the NHS and touched the hearts of millions around the globe. This selflessness and commitment to making the world a better place has a special place in the history of the UK, which currently ranks fourth in the global philanthropic league table.

In business, where the primary goal centres around profit-making, it's important to reflect on the role of altruism. Some entrepreneurs focus on quick gains, and subscribe to a 'pump and dump' philosophy, where philanthropy takes a back seat. However, this perspective is not universally accepted. The true essence of a company is multi-dimensional, transcending mere financial gains. In this view, the values of kindness and empathy hold equal significance in the pursuit of long-term success.

A company that sees its role as part of a broader, compassionate ecosystem aligns more closely with the values of its employees and customers. A sense of purpose can invigorate a business, instilling life and vigour into the colleagues that constitute its core. People, whether they are employees, clients, or the community at large, want to be part of a company that genuinely cares for others. Authentic corporate philanthropy, when thoughtfully embedded within a company's culture, can yield a profound impact on the communities it serves and the lives it touches.

Numerous examples of remarkable philanthropy exist within the business world. Companies such as Bruntwood, a commercial property specialist, generously allocate 10 per cent of their annual profits to charity. The values of equality, culture, and the environment are not just catchphrases but integral to every decision Bruntwood makes. Similarly, Greggs, the beloved high street bakers, extends their philanthropic initiatives to over 600 school breakfast clubs across the nation, ensuring that children have a nourishing start to their day. Furthermore, they focus on supporting communities in their northern English heartland, providing vital assistance to those facing financial hardship.

There are various ways for companies to give back, ranging from financial donations to volunteering at local initiatives. However, when philanthropy becomes a fundamental pillar of the business's identity, it not only enriches the lives of those outside the organization but also enhances its reputation as an employer of choice. Customers are discerning, and they tend to gravitate toward companies that display genuine care and social responsibility.

For Timpson, our commitment to giving back takes shape through the Timpson Foundation, our philanthropic arm. The foundation is built on three core objectives that we wholeheartedly support. Our charity match scheme is straightforward: we match pound for pound, up to £250, for every colleague who raises money for a charity of their choice and personally partic-ipates in the effort. This encourages active participation and showcases our dedication to charitable causes.

Our second initiative focuses on funding the recruitment, training, and employment of disadvantaged individuals across the UK. Over 10 per cent of our colleagues have joined our team through this pathway, including ex-offenders, veterans, and care leavers. This investment may be substantial, but it pays off manifold by introducing highly talented and dedicated individuals into our workforce.

By prioritizing kindness and generosity, businesses can build a virtuous circle that benefits from increased customer and staff loyalty, while supporting the communities they serve. These initiatives not only have a positive impact on the people they touch but also contribute to the businesses' growth and success. They serve as a testament to the power of generosity and compassion in transforming businesses into beacons of hope in their communities.

Last year, the Prison Reform Trust received a remarkable donation of £50,000 from an anonymous donor. The story behind this donation is as inspiring as it is heartwarming. A 24-year-old man who wished to remain anonymous decided to make a substantial contribution to this cause. His employer had a policy of matching bonus payments with donations to a charity of their choice. His choice was the Prison Reform Trust, and his generous act of kindness highlighted the potential for businesses to make a significant impact on society through charitable initiatives.

While political donations are often prominently featured in a company's accounts, information about charitable donations may be tucked away in less visible sections. To make generosity more visible and to encourage businesses to actively showcase their commitment to social causes, we should introduce a new practice. Alongside figures on sales and profits, the front page of a company's accounts should highlight charitable contributions. By doing so, we can underscore the importance of these contributions and their value in building a more compassionate society.

We should take pride in how caring companies contribute to society, not just through the profits they earn and the taxes they pay, but by the meaningful support they provide to those in need. Genuine philanthropy, when executed effectively, is not just good for business and the country; it is also a source of immense joy and fulfilment. It represents a commitment to giving back, enriching lives, and fostering a sense of community, ultimately creating a more compassionate and inclusive world.

PROVIDING SUPPORT BEFORE IT GOES WRONG

A concerning statistic from the Office for National Statistics, which details how 1 in 7 care leavers (15 per cent) will go on to receive a custodial sentence before the age of 24 underscores the importance of supporting care leavers in their transition to adulthood. Many care leavers face a higher risk of ending up in the criminal justice system, often experiencing a cycle of offending and imprisonment. These challenges are rooted in their disadvantaged backgrounds, marked by a lack of emotional and financial support networks. It is this alarming trend that highlights the critical role that organizations like the Timpson Foundation play in breaking this cycle, and giving care leavers a chance to lead meaningful and productive lives.

Timpson's participation in the Care Leaver Covenant (launched nationally in 2018) is a significant step towards addressing this issue. By offering care leavers valuable work experience in welcoming and inclusive environments, we aim to provide an alternative path. The work experience program, spanning two weeks, gives care leavers a glimpse into the world of retail. Through hands-on exposure, these young individuals have an opportunity to explore various skills, and gain insight into what it's like serving the public.

Perhaps most crucially, Timpson goes beyond offering work experience, and extends a lifeline to care leavers. After their placement, Timpson promises to provide job interviews to any care leaver interested in building a career within the Timpson Group. Once successfully onboarded, these colleagues receive a comprehensive 16-week training program, marked by unwavering support from their area teams. The training doesn't stop here; it continues throughout their careers, with various internal training courses available year-round.

This multi-pronged approach not only offers practical skills but also helps to instill a sense of purpose, belonging, and self-worth in care leavers. By inspiring and mentoring these individuals, Timpson seeks to set them on a path towards self-sufficiency, and a life free from the cycle of offending and imprisonment. This is the underlying ethos behind our participation in the Care Leaver Covenant. It is a commitment to nurturing brighter futures for young people who, with the right support and opportunities, can contribute positively to society, rewriting the narratives that once seemed inescapable.

In doing so, Timpson not only transforms the lives of these care leavers but also paves the way for a society that believes in second chances, inclusivity, and empowerment. Through their dedication and investment in these young individuals, Timpson is making a meaningful difference, reducing the risk of care leavers becoming trapped in a cycle of offending and imprisonment, and offering a path towards a brighter and more hopeful future.

How can we give back to our community?

Whatever initiative you opt for as a business, it is important that you choose an expression of the company's commitment to giving back that aligns with your own culture and needs, whether it be contributing to positive social impact, or fostering goodwill among employees and customers. Below, you'll find a number of ways in which you too can give back to the wider community.

Corporate matching programs

Implement a corporate matching program where the company matches the charitable donations raised by employees. This not only amplifies the impact of individual contributions but also encourages employees to give back.

Paid volunteer time

Offer paid volunteer time to employees, allowing them to engage in charitable activities during work hours. This demonstrates the company's support for community involvement and encourages employees to participate.

Community engagement committees

Establish community engagement committees comprised of employees. These committees can identify local causes, organize events, and manage philanthropic efforts, ensuring that charitable activities align with the company's values.

Donation drives

Organize donation drives for items like clothing, food, school supplies, or toys. Employees can contribute, and the company can facilitate the distribution of these donations to local charities.

Skills-based volunteering

Encourage employees to offer their professional skills to charitable organizations. This can involve providing free workshops, consulting, and the use of your facilities or other services, based on the employees' expertize.

Employee-selected charities

Allow employees to nominate and select charities or causes that are meaningful to them. The company can then allocate a budget to support these charities.

Corporate philanthropic events

Host corporate philanthropic events, such as charity runs, funfairs, or auctions. These events can involve employees, clients, and partners, raising funds for charitable causes.

Cause-related marketing
Launch products or campaigns with a promise to donate a portion of the sales to a chosen charity. This not only drives customer engagement but also contributes to social causes.

Community grants
Establish a community grants program to provide financial support to local non-profits, schools, or grassroots initiatives. This can help address specific community needs effectively.

Educational initiatives
Promote educational initiatives that support local schools or educational organizations. This can include scholarships, mentorship programs, or resource donations for schools in underserved areas.

Environmental sustainability
Develop and implement sustainable practices within the company, such as reducing waste, conserving energy, and supporting eco-friendly causes. Demonstrating commitment to the environment can be a form of philanthropy.

Support employee fundraising
Encourage and support employees who engage in personal fundraising efforts for charitable events like marathons, charity walks, or volunteer trips.

Local art and culture
Contribute to local art and culture by sponsoring events, artists, or cultural institutions. This can enrich the community's cultural landscape and promote creativity.

Engage with local causes
Identify and engage with local causes that align with the company's values and objectives. Building long-term partnerships with these causes can make a substantial impact.

Diversity and inclusion
Implement diversity and inclusion initiatives that support underrepresented groups in the workplace. This can involve diversity training, mentorship programs, and equal opportunity employment.

Customer engagement
Engage customers in philanthropic efforts. For instance, the company can donate a percentage of a customer's purchase to a selected charity.

Transparency and reporting
Maintain transparency in philanthropic activities. Provide regular reports on the impact of charitable efforts, both internally and externally.

Employee giving campaigns
Organize employee giving campaigns to raise funds for specific charitable initiatives, such as disaster relief efforts or long-term community projects. (Just like Captain Tom!)

Mentorship programs

Create mentorship programs that enable employees to support and guide disadvantaged individuals, whether they are young students, job seekers, or aspiring entrepreneurs.

Each of these initiatives, when executed thoughtfully, contributes to a culture of giving and social responsibility within the company. By fostering community engagement, promoting empathy, and supporting meaningful causes, companies can strengthen their bonds with employees and customers while making a positive impact on society.

Our commitment goes beyond delivering quality services and extends to our dedicated schemes designed to give directly back to the communities we serve.

One of our most notable initiatives is providing free dry-cleaning services for unemployed people and students attending their first interview. We recognize that these crucial moments can be life-changing, and we want to ensure that these job seekers have clean and presentable clothing to boost their confidence, and increase their chances of success in securing that job.

The free books written by my father, John, that are readily available in any of our branches are another way in which we encourage personal growth and education within the wider community. The books – *A Guide to Mental Health at Work, How to Create a Positive Future, A Guide to Attachment, Looking After Looked-After Children* and *A Guide to Teen Mental Health* – cover a diverse range of subjects and offer quick and easy-to-digest information for anyone in need of guidance or support.

Setting up the Alex Timpson Trust, in memory of my mother who passed away in 2016, is another pillar of our community support. By placing charity boxes in each of our shops, we actively collect money to fund holidays for foster families, and support research into how schools can better assist children in care. This initiative continues the legacy established by my mother, who dedicated her life to helping over 90 children shine. Through these charity boxes, we are continuing her work, and creating a positive impact on the lives of those in need. The simple idea of foregoing charges for small jobs and asking customers to contribute has been a win-win approach for everyone involved.

HOW TO MANAGE THE HIRING OF EX-OFFENDERS

It took a series of misfires for us to realize that not every ex-offender would be immediately work-ready following release. Alongside our Cobbler Algorithm and personality criteria, we have had to implement some company criteria to get around this issue.

We don't employ ex-offenders who have committed certain crimes (e.g. sex offences), remain unremorseful, or suffer from serious health problems. Most colleagues working for us who have been released committed acquisitive or drug-related offences, and are often from a care background. This initial screening is vital to ensure the safety and wellbeing of both colleagues and the public. It also ensures that candidates align with the core values of Timpson.

To further assist the return to work, we use a combination of the below schemes here at Timpson.

Release on Temporary Licence (ROTL)

A unique initiative that enables serving prisoners who are nearing the end of their sentences to leave prison every day to work in the community. The day release program offers a bridge between custody and release, allowing inmates to prepare for their gradual integration back into society. At Timpson, many ROTL colleagues leave prison every morning, complete a day's work in one of the company's shops, and return to their cell at the end of the working day. This scheme has proven a huge success, creating a smooth transition for these individuals as they return to the workforce upon release. We have one colleague in such a position who's currently running one of our busiest shops!

Prison training academies

We have invested in several specialist training academies, all of which are located within prison premises. These academies provide prisoners with practical training to better prepare them for employment upon release, reducing the likelihood of reoffending. The training academies mirror the services offered by Timpson's High Street stores (bar key cutting, for obvious reasons), enabling prisoners to gain valuable skills. Once released, they are fully skilled and prepared to join the Timpson or Max Photo teams, helping restore confidence and self-esteem.

The approach has been proven effective in helping ex-offender colleagues transition smoothly into the workplace, and it has been emulated by other leading firms, demonstrating the impact of vocational training and a supportive environment on reducing re-offending rates. At Timpson, we have an employee-retention rate of approximately 84 per cent, which is a testament to the hard work each one of us put into any individual's reintegration into society.

Recruitment teams

Our commitment to offering second chances is supported by two colleagues who visit around 70 prisons each year. Their role is to mentor and interview candidates for employment upon release. These interviews are short and focus exclusively on personality – considering factors like whether the candidate is open about their conviction, remorseful, good with people, and demonstrates a willingness to learn. By focusing on these key traits, which we hope all colleagues at Timpson have, we aim to identify the individuals who are genuinely committed to reintegrating into society, and contributing their newly learned skills.

A home for every colleague

If a new colleague doesn't have a place to live after release, we will find them a home and pay the deposit for them. In providing stable housing, and having on-hand financial support from other members of the team, we aim to build the foundations for successful reintegration into society, and long-term employment. Housing instability is a common challenge faced by ex-offenders, which is why we have this policy written into our hiring policy of ex-offenders.

Financial assistance

The financial assistance scheme is for all colleagues, ensuring that every member of our team has the resources they need to manage their daily expenses and tackle any financial challenges. Financial stability can significantly contribute to the successful reintegration of ex-offenders into society.

It is the championing of their personality, and the trust placed in our colleagues, based on the individuals they have become, that represent the distinctive heartbeat of our philosophy. Our slogan – Great Service by Great People – is all that counts here. We are looking to hire the person they are now, not who they once were.

Our hiring of ex-offenders, and the schemes we've put in place to support them, allow us to truly see our approach of upside-down management in action. We listen to the needs of everyone we hire and implement the support they need. Once you're hired, we treat you exactly the same as everyone else and there is no judgement, as we value their personalities and insights throughout their employment journey, just like everyone else.

This approach gives us the opportunity to build powerful relationships between our colleagues, the customers we serve, and the communities that we aim to improve. Today, we proudly employ many ex-offenders who have gone on to enjoy successful careers within the company and elsewhere. In offering opportunities and support to those who are trying to rebuild their lives, we are contributing to safer communities, lower rates of recidivism, and increased overall wellbeing.

What Have We Learned?

Transformative power of second chances

In hiring ex-offenders, you have access to a massive pool of talent that you might not necessarily think of when looking to bring on new members of the team. Statistics reveal that employment significantly reduces reoffending rates, creates safer communities, and breaks the cycle of crime.

Advocating for rehabilitation and reintegration

In focusing on mental health support and providing people – regardless of their status – with the tools they need in order to successfully reintegrate into society, you will benefit not only the individuals you aim to help but also serve the wider community with compassion.

Giving back to the community increases happiness

By giving your colleagues the support they need in order to help charities that they feel passionate about, whether through matching what they donate or giving them time to volunteer in the wider community, you will find that your company not only serves and supports the interests of your immediate team but also gives greater help to those who need it.

Invest in training

By investing in training early on, whether for care leavers, ex-offenders, students, those making a career change and more, you will find that the people you invest in will want to offer their support to the wider business and the communities they serve.

Similarly, if we take the negative cycle of release, reoffend, reincarcerate, you'll find that this early investment can shift an individual's perspective to one that focuses on learning, training and volunteering, which means everyone benefits from that initial bit of funding.

BRINGING IT ALL TOGETHER

Over the course of these past eight lessons, we have looked at everything from the importance of recruiting outside of traditional employment pools and avoiding business jargon in favour of simplicity, to looking outwardly at competitors and understanding the benefits of giving money away in order to receive more in the long run. Wherever you are right now as a company or as an individual, the key learnings and tactics discussed in this book will help you in bringing elements of an upside-down mindset to your own company. It has certainly worked for us!

As you embark on your journey towards building a thriving company, it's crucial to understand that this path is not linear. You'll encounter challenges, setbacks, and unexpected opportunities. The road to success is a winding trail with its share of surprises. However, it's in navigating these twists and turns that you'll learn the most valuable lessons. It's OK to say, 'I've messed up' and for your team to know that they can make mistakes too. It's part of the process of creating a great company built on a desire to always think of ways to improve, expand or remodel it.

Remember, your journey is unique and so is your company. What works for one business might not work for another, and that's perfectly fine. That's life. The key here is to adapt these lessons to your specific circumstances, while staying true to your company's vision and values.

When I think about setting goals and intentions for our business, I think about New Year's resolutions, a timeless tradition that has spanned generations. In the early days, this celebration extended over a 12-day festival where individuals made commitments to settle debts and return borrowed items, just as in business when the fiscal year comes to an end, and we must settle our taxes as well as pay any outstanding costs. Unlike a resolution though, your customers won't be happy if you don't honour their purchases. Never mind the suppliers who you rely on to successfully operate your business.

The University of Scranton conducted a survey that shows a relatively low 43 per cent of individuals set goals for themselves at the beginning of each year, and perhaps even more disheartening is that 23 per cent abandoned their New Year's resolutions within the first week. The pursuit of personal objectives, often centred around exercise, healthier eating habits, financial savings, and weight loss, can be a challenging commitment. Some people pledge to give Dry January a go, or commit to hill running at 6 a.m. each morning, only to find themselves falling off the wagon and reverting to their old ways, despite knowing that such ambition doesn't quite match up with their initial enthusiasm.

In **Lesson Three** (page 85), we discussed the importance of embracing changes that benefit your company, whether they are new modes of operation or a change in culture. But, like a failed resolution, the ability to regroup after it's not quite gone to plan is the best way forward. It's not just about adapting; it's about bouncing back stronger than before.

When you start a company, you always think it will be the best, most successful venture out there. If you encounter a setback and get through it that is a measure of your ability to win. You might lose out on a big pitch or find that the technology you're using isn't quite up to the standard you would expect. In response to these common issues in business, you may well get through somewhat unscathed but – just as with Dry January or hill running – if you encounter issue after issue that initial bout of confidence may begin to falter and those little missteps could turn into something much bigger and much more costly. So, if you can't quite find yourself getting out of bed early enough in the morning to head for your run or something in your personal life distracts you from your ultimate goal, it is time to reassess and think about what other measures you can put in place to help you on your journey to success. It is impossible to do everything on your own, which is why it is crucial to have a support network to help you along your way. You can't do everything on your own in your personal life, which is exactly the same in business.

Resilience is a quality that every leader must possess. It's what keeps you and your colleagues going when times are tough. It's what helps you rise above challenges and emerge triumphant. And it's not just for your sake; it's for your team's benefit too. Resilient leaders inspire and, crucially, build resilient teams. Whenever you face obstacles, remember that they are opportunities in disguise. Every setback is a chance to grow, to learn, and to come back even stronger.

I champion for the establishment of clear objectives and the formulation of well-considered plans in the workplace, which allows the dedication of the entire team in achieving them. It is my belief that well-intentioned goals, built around kindness, and well thought out, hold the key to a brighter future. Just as individuals require meaningful goals and well-defined plans, businesses also thrive when they set forth their aspirations, transparently communicating them to all within the company. As I said in **Lesson Two** (page 47), by building a company, and a culture, which gives benefits that go above and beyond financial contribution, you will find that the people you work with find true value in their commitment to the wider business. What good is a meticulously devised plan if your colleagues fail to grasp it or invest their belief in it? And remember, not everyone is interested in you achieving your goals. When they have their own too, that can be very different.

The most accomplished businesspeople that I've met throughout my career have always spoken of their commitment to their goals, routinely updating their to-do lists as they learn from past mistakes and look to inspiration from external sources, whether they are from companies, industries, or individuals that they aspire to emulate in their own lives. Further to that, these people continually add new goals to their list after accomplishing the ones they initially set out to achieve. In my own approach, I am inspired by the people I meet, the books I read and, most frequently, the ideas that come from the insights of my brilliant colleagues. Our business has flourished through the implementation of a straightforward mosaic of successful concepts, sourced both from within and beyond our company.

I've yet to meet another entrepreneur who doesn't see the glass as half-full and exude confidence in their capacity to enhance their businesses, even when facing tough headwinds.

Annually, I meet up with a few other entrepreneurs to discuss the year ahead, and what we are most looking forward to doing. Notably, our conversations do not tend to revolve around turnover or profit-driven goals. Instead, our emphasis – like everything I have said throughout this book – focuses on the core values that embody our respective businesses. Time and again, history has proven that when those foundational aspects are well-nurtured throughout the entire business, strong financial performance naturally occurs.

The majority of the people around the table also tend to discuss the pitfalls of significant errors and strategies to avert catastrophic mishaps. The wisest advice, although undeniably challenging to heed, is when it's time to pull the plug on a business or an idea that isn't yielding the results you anticipated. The first loss is always the cheapest. If we can be consistently candid with ourselves, acknowledging when our capabilities fall short of our self-perceived excellence, we could save a fortune, and reduce our stress levels in the process. (Remember, 95 per cent of the job in being a leader is saying 'no'.)

When it was my turn to share, I contemplated outlining our plans for addressing an ongoing recruitment challenge in a specific area of the UK, or our strategy for expanding the presence of our photo ID booths. However, I opted to focus on the two core objectives that I am continually refining, along with a new one.

My primary objectives are to instil greater kindness in our business and to continually increase happiness among our colleagues. These two goals represent the essence of our company culture and inform our day-to-day operations. By consistently enhancing our commitment to these values, we can expect to see an ever-increasing number of satisfied customers returning to us, and happy colleagues with smiles on their faces.

At the heart of our business are the people, of course, and then there's the culture, which reaches back to the generations that managed the family business before me, those who helped it on its way to becoming the company that it is today, which I am incredibly privileged to continue to look after.

The duties that go into leading a company, and the pressures of being responsible for the lives of your colleagues and their families, as well as the wider business, can be a lot of pressure. By following the techniques outlined over the course of these lessons you will be able to create and build a company that is not only financially successful, but consistently puts the people who you work with at its core.

Putting it all into practice

Perhaps you are just starting out and want to know what your core values are, or maybe you have just taken on a new role in a company and want to bring some new energy to it. If it's either of these, or anything between, look back at what we have discussed and see what you can apply to your business, where it is now, and start to action that change. Set those goals, continually adapt them, and work together with the team to make them happen.

Let's say that you have just started at a company, and you are leading its expansion. You want to make sure that you are bringing in the best people to champion the ambitions and vision of the people who hired you, but you don't know where to start. Well, like with everything I have discussed throughout the course of this book, it should be done with a focus on simplicity.

Begin assessing the morale of the team and if you can't work out what they are thinking or how they operate, ask them. The best ideas come from those on the front line. Sometimes what they say may be uncomfortable to hear, but their suggestions need to be heard, and their ideas (if they're any good) should be put into practice. They may not be high-level strategic ideas, but it will help make the day-to-day operations work more effectively, giving you the time and money to focus on the strategy of the business and achieving your company goals. In the first few weeks of your job take our Happy Index (see page 88) and modify it to suit your own needs, but remember, it should be simple and restricted to just one question, with a select number of easy-to-understand responses that your fellow team members can answer to provide you with a fuller picture, which can then be further drilled down into to fully appreciate and evaluate their response

If you can't quite work out why some tasks aren't getting finished on time, ask the question: *Do you feel that you can always finish your daily duties within working hours?*

On a scale of 1–10, do you feel that you can always finish your daily duties within working hours?

Please tick the appropriate box (1–6 is poor, 7–8 is average, 9–10 is excellent)

	1	2	3	4	5	6	7	8	9	10
Time										

If the responses are all negative, you know that there's a problem with the workload, time management, or the people. It's then about looking at which processes are taking away the time and focus from the team. Perhaps there are two, three, or even four sign-off decisions to be made before something can be approved among the wider team and rolled out throughout the company. If so, there is clearly a lack of trust in the culture you've taken on. Maybe someone in the team isn't as number-savvy as the rest and needs some additional support. But of course, this is all guesswork unless you investigate. To get to the heart of the matter you need to be open and have the difficult conversations.

Here's how we'd do it at Timpson.

Workload

Start by assessing the processes, daily practices, and key criteria that need to be accomplished before Person A can move on to the next task, and ask each member of the team the below questions:

1. Is this a necessary function of the job?
2. How much does it cost?
3. Do you spend more time on this than you should?

The reason for asking these questions of the team that you are trying to 'fix' is simple, they know the ins and outs of the business better than you do. They will, more often than not, have bucketloads of ideas that will ultimately streamline and improve the processes that are adding to their workload, and save the company cash and increase productivity among the entire team.

You need to be decisive and let the people who understand the technology, service, or whatever it may be tell you the issue. If it is haemorrhaging overheads and there's a simpler way to do things, do it. If multiple people are spending more time checking and rechecking things when they don't have to, move that responsibility across to one person who understands it best. If anyone on the team says that the function is an additional measure but not necessary to their role, scrap it immediately. In every team there will be colleagues who know the answers, it's your job to find, develop and support them to allow you all to achieve the aims of the business.

Leadership is about making quick decisions, and it is also about making sure you are listening to the wider team. Maybe scrapping that function will be a mistake but you won't know unless you give it a try. You are all in this together, and by trying new things, you will often find a better path for efficiently and quickly crossing off the to-dos from your list.

Time management
Generally speaking, time management goes hand-in-hand with an individual's workload, but it doesn't have to.

If you remove unnecessary steps from processes and give autonomy to your team, you will see productivity spike almost immediately.

A rigid working structure is good when it is paramount to the successful delivery of a project, but it can slow progress if you need to factor in approvals from senior members of the team. Approval processes have their place, but they are often instigated by a finance director to stop a one-off problem from happening again. This added complexity can often cost far more than it was ever meant to save.

People

Now, this is more of a nuanced issue, and will require you to peel back the layers from your findings about the team's workload and time-management skills. If, despite trying brand-new ideas and cutting down on unnecessary measures, you are still finding failings within the team, it's time to look at the people you are working with.

Like I said in **Lesson One** (page 13), assembling a high-performing Super Team should be focused on an individual's personality and their alignment with the company culture but, crucially, also eventuate whether they will help the wider company. Every team requires a mixture of those positive attributes that I discussed on page 27. You don't want to have a Mr Dull working with a Mrs Determined. It could drastically change the team dynamics, and have a negative impact on Mrs Determined, the colleague committed to the company's goals and the person who exemplifies your internal culture. Focus your efforts on the 9s and 10s.

Have another look at the team and identify their key qualities, how they work and what they bring to the business, then put their name or initials by the qualities you are looking for, especially those that fit into the personality traits.

Once you have done these things, it's time to look at your findings with a fresh pair of eyes.

If the dynamics of the team aren't working, be honest and open with the team. Should a member of the team be better suited to another function, ask them what they want and, of course, if they feel comfortable swapping roles, and then make it happen. It's often kinder and better for the company, as a whole, if the people working in specific teams and roles are happy and content; if they're not, it's fine to make alternative arrangements and reassess.

After you've done your due diligence, it might, now, be time to have that difficult conversation with a colleague who isn't good enough for the business. As you know, I don't find these conversations easy, but by sticking to the facts, and ensuring that the person in question isn't made to feel less than their colleagues, you can often find an arrangement that benefits everyone in the team. Just as I advised in **Lesson Six** (page 169), having open communication and trusting your colleagues to be honest, both with you and themselves, can be a transformative experience for your team and the wider company.

When you approach these conversations with empathy and transparency, it's possible to arrive at solutions that suit everyone involved. Keep in mind that every team member's wellbeing and professional growth are essential elements of your company's success.

It's also worth considering mentorship and coaching opportunities. If you have team members who excel in certain areas, encourage them to share their knowledge and skills with others. This not only supports their personal growth but also contributes to the overall strength of the team.

In bringing the power of gratitude into your leadership style (turn to page 191), so that you can think about counting your pebbles) you not only create a happier and more motivated team but also strengthen the bonds that hold your company together.

During your journey in the workplace, no matter the position, remember that the path is not always linear, and challenges are bound to arise. But with an open heart, a commitment to personal growth, and a dedication to your team, you can build a company that thrives both financially and emotionally.

By creating a workplace where kindness and colleague wellbeing are paramount, you're not only fostering the success of your business but also shaping a world where the values you hold dear have a meaningful impact.

Look back to **Lesson Two** (see page 47) and think about the ways in which you can maintain a positive culture that has its people at the core. If you build it, if you lead that change, and make sure it's at the heart of every single colleague's commitment, you are on to a winner.

It's crucial to have a system for measuring your progress. How do you know if you're effectively applying these lessons in your business? It's not just about achieving financial success; it's about ensuring that your company is aligned with your values and making a positive impact on your team and the wider community.

Consider setting key performance indicators (KPIs) that align with the principles discussed in these lessons. These KPIs should reflect not only financial metrics but also those related to employee wellbeing, customer satisfaction, and community engagement. Regularly tracking and evaluating these metrics – with simplicity – will help you stay on the right path, and make the necessary adjustments when pertinent. If you can't write them all on a match box, the list is too long.

The essence of running a business

Business is a landscape that is constantly in flux, but the lessons I've shared with you are timeless yet adaptable. They form the foundation of an upward trajectory for any company, from fledgling start-ups to established organizations seeking a reboot. I hope you find as much insight in this book as I have found in the many I've read since I started in business.

As you reflect on these lessons and consider how to apply them in your unique circumstances, remember that one of the most powerful attributes a company and leader can possess is adaptability. The world changes all the time, and the ability to pivot, innovate, and continuously learn is essential for success. If my great-great-grandfather could see our family business today, he wouldn't recognize anything similar to the one he ran, bar the name above the door and the essence of a caring company. Businesses change all the time, some close while others thrive. The ones where the leaders have their eyes open to change are the ones that tend to do best.

The essence of running a business, as I've come to understand it, can be distilled into a few key principles.

Lead with kindness

In a world often driven by profit margins and cut-throat competition, kindness can sometimes seem like a weakness. However, I stand by the belief that kindness is the most potent tool a leader and company can wield. By genuinely caring for your team, and fostering a culture of respect and compassion, you lay the foundation for lasting success.

Set clear goals

Like the New Year's resolutions that many of us struggle to maintain, clear and well-defined goals are the cornerstones of progress and innovation. Your goals should inspire and motivate your team, offering a vision of what your company can become. As you strive to meet these goals, reflect on the wisdom of past mistakes, and seek inspiration from the world around you. Any business goals should always have the company's aims at their heart.

Learn from others

The most successful individuals I've met throughout my career have one thing in common – they are always learning. Be open to new ideas, whether they come from your colleagues, books, podcasts, or the broader world. Just as our business has grown through the assimilation of successful concepts, you too can embrace a wealth of knowledge that will improve your company's performance.

Embrace practicality

Leadership and colleague happiness is not about grandiose gestures or abstract theories; it's about making practical decisions that serve your company and its people. Whether it's cutting unnecessary processes, streamlining operations, or facilitating open and honest conversations within your team, practicality and speed should be your guiding lights.

Recognize the right time

The most challenging decisions a leader faces often involve recognizing when it's time to let go. Whether it's a business idea that's not giving you the results, a colleague who might be happier elsewhere, or a process that's more trouble than it's worth, the first loss is often the cheapest.

Value unconventional wisdom
Sometimes, success can be found where others are not looking. Investing in unglamorous, overlooked sectors can result in surprising profits. Don't follow the crowd blindly; seek opportunities where others may not be looking.

Peel back the layers
When facing team challenges, don't just scratch the surface. Dive deep into the intricacies of workload, time management, and individual strengths. Ask questions, involve your team in problem-solving, and be open to the possibility that an unconventional solution might be the key to success.

Prioritize wellbeing
Your team's happiness and wellbeing are not just nice-to-haves; they are essential drivers of your company's success. Lead with empathy and transparency, encourage mentorship and coaching, and make sure every team member feels valued and supported each and every day.

Embrace change
Finally, as you continue your journey, remember that change is a constant. The business world evolves, and your ability to adapt and innovate will be the difference between stagnation and growth.

I hope these principles help guide you well on your path, whatever it may be. It's been an honour to share these lessons with you, and I'm confident that with kindness, clear goals, practicality, and a commitment to your team's wellbeing that you can create a company that thrives both financially and emotionally.

Just as our family's business has stood the test of time by putting people at its core, you too can shape a world where your values have a meaningful impact. Leading a business is not just a role; it's a responsibility that allows you to nurture a culture that values individuals, purpose, and heart. By embodying these principles, you have the potential to not only make a mark in your industry, but also leave a lasting legacy of leadership and kindness for the generations that follow.

As we move to the conclusion of this book, remember that the journey to building a thriving company is always ongoing. It doesn't have a final destination; it's a continuous cycle of growth, learning, and adaptation. Embrace change, innovation, and kindness as integral parts of your company's DNA.

Continue seeking inspiration from various sources. Don't underestimate the power of learning from those around you; they hold valuable insights and experiences that can fuel your company's growth.

So, whether you're a new manager embarking on a leadership journey, or an established colleague seeking to breathe new energy into your company, embrace these lessons, set meaningful goals, and work together with your team to make them happen. In the end, it's not just about heading a company; it's about leading with vision and heart.

Continue to lead and work with a purpose, and the future is full of potential and promise.

15 BOOKS THAT ARE VALUABLE FOR ALL BUSINESS LEADERS

The Richer Way by Julian Richer

The Richer Way was the first business book I ever read that gave me the confidence to run the business in a way that felt aligned with my values. It was a clear guide on how to motivate people through kindness and fun.

The Ethical Capitalist by Julian Richer

The Ethical Capitalist is a step on from *The Richer Way*, making a clear argument that you don't have to be a 'tough boss' to make money. In fact, the most profitable companies over the long term are those with strong values and a clear purpose.

Dear James by John Timpson

This was written by my dad as a way of explaining to others how our culture of upside-down management works, and it became a great guide to our colleagues as they developed their careers in the company. It's still a good seller!

Parkinson's Law by C Northcote Parkinson

A wonderful little book, and while some of the chapters are off the mark by today's standards, the argument about the inefficiencies in organisations over time is spot on, and should be read by every leader and politician.

The Nordstrom Way to Customer Service Excellence
by Robert Spector

A similar book to *The Richer Way*, in that it sets out how a focus on amazing service results in a business that has a long-term future. Customers respond well to great service, and are prepared to pay that little bit extra for it.

Nuts! by Kelvin Freiburg

This book is all about Southwest Airlines and how one inspirational leader created a culture where they bucked the trend on how to run an airline, by focussing on a very small number of important factors . . . recruit great people, keep it simple, and focus on getting the planes in the sky. I've been to their offices in the states to see it for myself, and I've never seen a culture more aligned to ours at Timpson.

The Lego Story by Jens Andersen

I love how a family business has continued to innovate while sticking to its core products, values, and history. It is a company with confidence and hasn't lost focus while technology has changed their industry so dramatically.

The Yellow Earl: Almost an Emperor, Not Quite a Gentleman by Douglas Sutherland
> This book tells a story from a bygone era, where the Earl of Lonsdale, once the richest person in the country, lived a life no one could ever imagine today. It's not really about business but about confidence and the energy for adventure.

Titan: The Life of John D Rockefeller by Ron Chernow
> While I don't like his style of business, this long book is a fascinating business story, and one that to me showed that no matter what scale your business is, you need to keep focussed on growing, despite the barriers that are continually put in your way. Clearly an eccentric man, but an astute businessman who ended up being one of the world's greatest philanthropists.

Business As Usual by Anita Roddick
> Body Shop was, in its day, an incredible, values-led retailer that made great waves across the globe. Anita's focus on doing the right thing ahead of making money helped create not just a great company but a new movement in ethical retailing and sustainability. It also showed me that customers will choose you if they like your values. I'm sure if Anita was still alive today she would employ ex-offenders too.

Redeemable by Erwin James
> This book is written by a friend of mine who spent a long time in prison. Erwin, or Jim to his friends, has become a leading voice in prison reform, and he's a great communicator about the purpose of prison, and how hope is needed for the many

men and women locked up. His dream in prison was to have a small cottage with a fishpond in the garden. The last time we met we went fishing in his pond at the end of his garden.

McDonald's: Behind the Arches by John F Love

This is a must-read book for any aspiring business leader. It's a great way of seeing that a successful business always has high standards and sticks to what it does best. I'm a massive fan of their business model and international success, and one day hope to see their 'hamburger university'.

Good to Great by Jim Collins

This is a bible book for so many leaders, and sets the tone for a focus on being ambitious while maintaining simplicity and high standards.

Exceeding Customer Expectations: What Enterprise, America's #1 Car Rental Company, Can Teach You About Creating Lifetime Customers by Kirk Kazanjian

This is a book all about the Enterprise Rental Car business, and shows you that if you follow the pack you probably won't win, but if you think and do differently, and focus on amazing customer service, you probably will come out on top. I always try to use Enterprise when I can, as their service is always the best and I like supporting them – they still act like the underdog even though they are a multi-billion dollar business nowadays.

Grit *by Angela Duckworth*

A beacon for business leaders and colleagues, which reveals the transformative impact of passion and perseverance in the workplace. Combining research-backed wisdom, *Grit* empowers readers toward unparalleled achievement in all avenues of life, and is particularly useful for colleagues going through a difficult time. By cultivating individual grit, professionals foster a resilient mindset, driving productivity, and conquering challenges in both work and life. Duckworth's insights allow professionals to navigate the complexities of the business world with unwavering determination.

USEFUL LINKS AND ORGANIZATIONS

Samaritans
Contact: 116 123 (24/7 helpline)
Website: www.samaritans.org

Mind
Contact: 0300 123 3393
Website: www.mind.org.uk

Citizens Advice
Contact: 0800 144 8848 (England) 0800 702 2020 (Wales)
Website: www.citizensadvice.org.uk

Mental Health Foundation
Contact: info@mentalhealth.org.uk
Website: www.mentalhealth.org.uk

Mental Health at Work
Contact: 020 3553 3665
Website: www.mentalhealthatwork.com

Rethink Mental Illness
Contact: 0300 5000 927
Website: www.rethink.org

Acas (Advisory, Conciliation, and Arbitration Service)
Contact: 0300 123 1100
Website: www.acas.org

The Money Advice Service
Website: www.moneyhelper.org.uk

Turn2us
Contact: 0808 802 2000
Website: www.turn2us.org.uk

Macmillan Cancer Support
Contact: 0808 808 00 00
Website: www.macmillan.org.uk

Disability Rights UK
Contact: 0330 995 0400
Website: www.disabilityrightsuk.org

The Stroke Association
Contact: 0303 3033 100
Website: www.stroke.org.uk

Carers UK
Contact: 0808 808 7777
Website: www.carersuk.org

Age UK

Contact: 0800 678 1602

Website: www.ageuk.org.uk

Please note that contact details and operating hours may be subject to change, so it's advisable to check the websites of the organizations I have listed here for the most up-to-date information and support options.

ACKNOWLEDGEMENTS

My wife Roisin and I met at university, so she has known and supported me throughout my entire working life. The many nights I have been away working, with early morning starts, and the demands of business impacting our home life, have never been challenged. The advice I get from her is always considered and with others in mind, and without her influence the business wouldn't be as fun and happy as it is.

Our three children – Bede, Niamh, and Patrick – are also experienced in visiting shops while in their prams, and are now making their own way in the retail world. They have been exposed to the business all their lives, sometimes it has been too much looking back, but their support has been, and continues to be, humbling.

My mum Alex sadly died in 2016, too early to carry on her mission to help disadvantaged people with their lives. She taught me so many things, but maybe it's her irreverence for authority, and the fact that no one is more important than anyone else, that has given me the confidence to challenge the norm, and stick up for people who've had a difficult start in life.

ACKNOWLEDGEMENTS

My dad John and I have worked together for over 30 years. We have never argued, never disagreed, and to this day have the same values and vision for the business. We make a great team. He has also allowed me to be myself in the business, to try things, to fail and to win. We may be from different generations, but we have created a business that enables the family business to carry on for another five generations.

My colleagues are incredible. They embrace our culture, run the business how they see fit, support new colleagues as they start their journey, and show kindness to me and my family, often over their whole career.

I've been very fortunate to have Paresh Majithia as Finance Director for the last 20 years, who has embraced our culture, supported me when the financial risks often seemed high, and trusted my judgement when we have diversified away from basic cobbling. Everyone needs a numbers expert, but I've been lucky enough to find someone who is also a caring, empathetic leader.

Gouy Hamilton Fisher is our Director of Colleague Support, in most companies this is known as HR and People Director. Gouy is as cool as ice under pressure, he's brilliant at delivering good and bad news, and setting the standards on how we care and communicate with our colleagues. Every business needs a Gouy.

Janet Leighton is Director of Happiness, a slightly contradictory title as her time is mostly spent with colleagues who aren't happy. Instead they have personal problems that require her support and patience to get them back on the straight and narrow, and to ensure the benefits we give our colleagues are both used and appreciated.

Darren Burns spends much of his time in prisons, recruiting great colleagues and helping other employers start their journey with prison recruitment. He has been instrumental in supporting the business, from employing 100 ex-offenders to now over 600.

I couldn't have started my prison journey if it hadn't been for the kindness and willingness of prison governors, their teams, and their bosses at the Ministry of Justice. To this day they remain supportive and help move the many barriers that often come in our way.

Sid, Sue, Ann, Will, and Brent run our retail and direct businesses, and do so with kindness and an appreciation that their roles are to ensure our culture is cared for and our colleagues are happy.

Julian Richer is an inspiration and mentor to me. Julian founded a chain of hifi and audio shops across the UK, and wrote a book called *The Richer Way*. This book acted as a guidebook for me, helping me to understand how to run a business with culture and kindness at its core. We have remained good friends for many years, share ideas in a little pub near Julian's house in York every few months, and have common interests in human rights and justice. Julian took over from me at the *Sunday Times* as their new business columnist.

I've been proud to be Chair of the Prison Reform Trust (PRT) and lead a wonderful team of academics and prison experts who support prisoners and their families. I've learned a lot about how prisons work, and how best to support people whose lives are impacted by crime and the justice system. All proceeds from this book have been donated to PRT.

I extend my gratitude to the efforts of the brilliant publishing team at HarperNorth who played a pivotal role in making *The Happy Index* a reality. My editor, Ben McConnell, provided invaluable insights and unwavering support throughout the writing of this book with good humour and an unfaltering can-do attitude. Alice Murphy-Pyle and Taslima Khatun for spearheading the promotional efforts of the campaign. Charlotte Macdonald did an excellent job editing the text, ensuring that my words were crystal-clear. The excellent front cover was designed by the hugely talented Steve Leard and perfectly encapsulates the contents of the book. Thank you, too, to Jo Ireson for their diligent reading of the text. To the rest of the people from the sales, production, and rights departments at HarperCollins, I appreciate your collective effort and commitment to this project. Thank you for making *The Happy Index* a reality.

To Toby Mundy and the rest of the team at Aevitas Creative Management UK, thank you for finding a publishing house that saw the potential of *The Happy Index*.

Oli Shah works for the *Sunday Times* and suggested I write a weekly column about business and how we do things at Timpson. He allowed me to focus on corporate kindness and challenge the normal state of thinking in business today. The platform he gave me in turn led to the publication of this book. The *Sunday Times* team waived their rights to the content of the articles so we could use my columns in this book, and in doing so raise more money for PRT.

When I first became CEO I was lucky to join a business group called YPO. It stands for Young Presidents Organization, and while I'm now 52 and not so young, I'm still a member, and have been heavily influenced by the speakers and the friendships that Roisin and I have been fortunate enough to listen and learn from over many years. My forum are incredible business leaders, and many of the ideas we've added to the business have come from them.

Finally, I would like to thank our customers. Over 500,000 people a week choose to come to our shops, and in doing so support my colleagues, and in turn help us support others.

INDEX

INDEX

Harper North

would like to thank the following staff and contributors for their involvement in making this book a reality:

Fionnuala Barrett
Samuel Birkett
Peter Borcsok
Ciara Briggs
Katie Buckley
Sarah Burke
Alan Cracknell
Jonathan de Peyer
Anna Derkacz
Tom Dunstan
Kate Elton
Sarah Emsley
Simon Gerratt
Monica Green
Natassa Hadjinicolaou
Jo Ireson
Megan Jones

Jean-Marie Kelly
Taslima Khatun
Steve Leard
Sammy Luton
Charlotte Macdonald
Rachel McCarron
Ben McConnell
Molly McNevin
Alice Murphy-Pyle
Adam Murray
Genevieve Pegg
Agnes Rigou
Florence Shepherd
Eleanor Slater
Emma Sullivan
Katrina Troy
Daisy Watt

For more unmissable reads,
sign up to the HarperNorth newsletter at
www.harpernorth.co.uk

or find us on Twitter at
@HarperNorthUK

**Harper
North**